SEX AND SPIRIT

What is the real magic behind "good sex"? How do some husbands and wives manage to keep their lovemaking ecstatically charged through a lifetime of deep relating? How can you personally attain continual spiritual rejuvenation through sexual intercourse? Delving into both the physical and spiritual dynamics of sexual relationships, *Peak Sexual Experience* explores key professional techniques and insights that can generate vast new realms of physical pleasure and spiritual fulfillment in your love life.

Included in this definitive text on sex and spirit are:
*Special breathing techniques for greater sexual power
*Anxiety-reducing programs for enhancing sexual pleasure
*Ways to lengthen and intensify actual orgasm
*Suggestions for deepening pre-intercourse intimacy
*Techniques for expanding verbal and visual intercourse
*Reflections on your past love affairs and present sexual desires
*Skin-to-skin spiritual meditations while making love
*Intimate pathways to intuitive heart contact during sex.

Designed to be read either on your own or with your lover, *Peak Sexual Experience* helps you awaken your potential for transcendent, mystical realms of sexual union—and shows you how such spiritual union during intercourse can enrich all aspects of your life.

Also by John Selby

SECRETS OF A GOOD NIGHT'S SLEEP
KUNDALINI AWAKENING IN EVERYDAY LIFE
IMMUNE SYSTEM ACTIVATION
BELLYTALK
FINDING EACH OTHER
CONSCIOUS HEALING

John Selby has studied the psychological and spiritual elements of sexual intimacy at Princeton, Berkeley, the San Francisco Theological Seminary, the Radix Institute, and research institutes throughout the world. He helped found the San Luis Obispo Wholistic Health Center, and has treated patients in private practice for sixteen years. He has written six other books on various aspects of intimacy.

Sex and Spirit:

Merging Heart and Soul in Love

John Selby

toExcel
San Jose New York Lincoln Shanghai

Sex and Spirit

This edition republished by arrangement with toExcel,
a strategic unit of Kaleidoscope Software, Inc.

For information address:
toExcel
165 West 95th Street, Suite B-N
New York, NY 10025
www.toExcel.com

ISBN: 1-58348-201-6

Library of Congress Catalog Card Number: 99-61359

Printed in the United States of America

0 9 8 7 6 5 4 3 2 1

*This book is dedicated to all of you who seek,
through your intimate erotic encounters,
a deeper sense of spiritual fulfillment
in life.*

CONTENTS

PREFACE

We all know from personal experience that there exists a vast and ultimately fulfilling spiritual dimension to sexual love. Occasionally in the middle of a wild erotic encounter, we suddenly find our hearts opening spontaneously in total vulnerability, nakedness, and trust with our lover—and we explode into an unbelievably beautiful state of total spiritual orgasm.

Everyone hungers to be blessed with this transcendent quality of earthly love on a regular basis, but in most bouts of lovemaking, true spiritual union is unfortunately seldom experienced. All our petty thoughts and worries, habitual inhibitions and emotional contractions thwart our attempts to share ecstatic spiritual communion with our lover.

The heart of this book is focused on the following question: Can we do nothing to augment the spiritual dimensions of lovemaking in our lives, or are there practical ways for encouraging mystic orgasm each and every time we dive into bed with our beloved? Put bluntly, can we learn to consciously awaken a sense of mystic communion right in the middle of our earthly pleasures?

There do exist remarkable pathways for deepening our mystic experience during intercourse. This book, drawn both from my professional work in marriage counseling and from several of the most potent spiritual traditions of sexual awakening, offers an intimate exploration of practical approaches for attaining peak sexual experience with your lover. You will find these approaches intensely pleasurable to explore as you learn ways to awaken the divine power of spiritual love right in the middle of an exploding physical orgasm.

Ancient religious traditions such as sexual Kung Fu in China, and the Kundalini couples-meditation tradition in Tibet, have taught ways for turning sexual intercourse into mystic awakening, where lovers directly experience the creative force of the universe as it manifests in the earthly process of physical love. This universal mystic experience is in many ways the ultimate spiritual act in life. Sexual intercourse is where we truly come closest to being gods ourselves as we participate in the ultimate creative process through which new beings are brought into the world.

Even though human sexual relating is obviously a communion with divine love and creation, all too often in our culture sexual passion has been seen as diametrically opposed to spiritual awakening. The ways of the flesh have been castigated rather than lauded, and subjected to antagonistic attacks by religious leaders. One of my early teachers, Alan Watts, in his book *Nature, Man and Woman*, has documented how sexuality in our own culture has been abused as an enemy of mystic communion rather than its intimate companion.

"How strange it is," he once said, "to teach youngsters that God is to be found way off in the sky somewhere beyond our earthly senses and passions, rather than right here in the middle of everyday life. Where are we to discover the nature of divine love, if not through sexual love?" In his lectures and writings, Alan regularly pointed out that we all must consciously strive daily toward the unification of our sexual and spiritual nature if we're to truly enter into the spiritual realms of being.

The purpose of this book is not to argue abstract theological points and conflicting religious dogma related to the relationship of sexuality and divine love. Instead, we're going to focus on the experiential dimensions of mystic communion during intercourse. All we need to agree on is that God is Love, and through sexual communion with our lover, we can expand into mystic union with our Creator.

The beautiful fact is that regardless of differing theological inclinations, we can all learn to tap directly into the immense mystic power that lies deep within each of us, awaiting the opportunity to rise up in the midst of sexual intercourse to transform sexual relating into spiritual communion. Whatever our particular religious affiliation or independent spiritual status, we can readily employ this book's understanding of how to awaken vast new spiritual depths in our marriage or love affair.

Both from psychological and spiritual points of view, there appear to be seven primary aspects to sexual relating that need to be reflected upon and consciously expanded in a love affair or marriage if we want to actively encourage the inflow of spiritual energies into our bouts of lovemaking. Each of these seven dimensions can open up remarkable new realms of ecstasy and sexual fulfillment.

In the intimate case studies presented in the pages to

come, we're going to see first-hand how loving couples learn to awaken a newfound sense of holy love during intercourse by tapping deeper into each of the seven dimensions of sexual relating. By hearing these experiences of everyday people as they open up to higher levels of peak sexuality, you'll discover for yourself how to apply these approaches to your own love life.

However, we should understand from the beginning that this book does not prescribe rote sexual techniques for spiritual awakening. In quite an opposite thrust, the seven programs you will learn are aimed at awakening a spontaneous, unpremeditated sense of sexual responsiveness in your relating. The final truth is that only through putting aside all mechanical techniques and quieting all efforts to achieve sexual ecstasy are we able to open up to truly mystic energies and heartfelt spiritual love in the heat of our sexual passions. We reach the peak of sexual communion when all thoughts, all techniques, all manipulations drop away, and we merge with the universal creative power that lies beyond our individual being.

I have witnessed over and over again in my marriage counseling that if a man and a woman cannot let go of their ego-thoughts and separate identities while making love, and surrender their hearts and bodies to the spiritual presence that pervades the universe, then hearts remain closed, relationships deteriorate, and loneliness looms on the horizon.

In this light, recent trends in our culture have often proven devastating to many sexual involvements because of the strong fixation on manipulation rather than surrender, on individual power rather than shared love. Now, as we progress through the nineties and into a new century, our great challenge is to learn realistic approaches for awakening the spirit of genuine intimacy and spiritual surrender in our sexual relationships, so that we gain that ultimate sense of total and unconditional union between our personal soul, the soul of our sexual partner, and the infinite spiritual presence that lies just beyond the boundary of our personal ego bubble.

A primary observation in my therapy work has been that the couples who stay together and also grow together are couples for whom the underlying spiritual dimension of sexuality comes vividly alive in their relationship. When spiritual love merges with sexual love, hearts become united, and relationships endure and deepen.

As said in an ancient Tibetan sexual text, "Infinite blessings flow into the lives of all who sacrifice individual isolation and plunge unafraid into the mysteries of total orgasmic union."

INTRODUCTION
Hungering for Spiritual Intimacy

Susan was finishing her degree in business administration when she fell wildly in love with Thomas. They got married a year later, and chose to continue advancing their separate careers. They bought a house and settled into what should have been a fulfilling life together. But even though they considered themselves quite sophisticated lovers and did all the right things with each other, as time went by they continued to feel somehow separate, unable to achieve a certain quality of intimate heart contact. Instead, they felt trapped inside their separate worlds, striving for sexual and spiritual closeness but never quite attaining it.

So many couples like Tom and Susan get caught up in the routines of their daily lives, manage to succeed on superficial levels, but come to realize that they are still trapped as isolated prisoners inside their own hearts, unable to break free of the invisible barriers that keep them from attaining genuine spiritual union with each other.

I have seen far too many such relationships with high potential for success suddenly hit the rocks and break hopelessly apart. However, in marriage counseling sessions, I have also witnessed many couples learning successfully to overcome the inhibitions that were blocking the true spiritual intimacy they were hungering for in their sexual relationship. It's always a great pleasure to see two sincere people open up to the greater powers of love that lie beyond mundane dimensions of sexual relating.

Tom and Susan were a prime example of a couple on the point of breaking up. Their friends, however, thought they were doing great together. They'd both managed, for instance, to power their way through the end of the eighties with quite notable successes in their business careers. They were able to buy all the things they wanted for their leisure time. They indulged in quite lavish trips during the holidays. And their parties were talked about for weeks afterward.

However, at a certain point Susan simply broke down, unable to pretend to herself any longer that she was satisfied with her relationship. She finally took honest stock of her emotional situation, and realized that she was feeling more lonely now in her married life than she had felt as a single girl back in college. Sometimes late at night when Tom was sound asleep beside her in bed, she even found herself resorting to her old habit of masturbation as she conjured up vague fantasies of a true love who would finally transport her into the spiritual realms of boundless ecstasy and mystic union she knew in her heart must exist.

She kept her feelings buried inside her for several weeks. Then one evening, she tried to share her feelings with Thomas. Instead of opening up to her painful but honest feelings, he immediately contracted, changing the direction of the conversation before she could even get started talking through her difficult emotions.

A few days later, she happened to see an announcement for one of my weekly intimacy groups that I offer in my community when time permits. On impulse, in order to gain some pragmatic inputs on what to do to improve her situation, she decided to attend the first meeting, even if it meant risking the embarrassment of admitting something was wrong with her relationship.

I could tell that she was acutely nervous sitting in the circle of twenty-five people in the room. I had listed this new group specifically as a sexual-intimacy group, and there seemed to be a prevailing anxiety in the circle that the group might turn out to be a sixties-style sexual orgy rather than the serious exploration of spiritual intimacy that most of the participants were seeking.

The very notion of attending an intimacy group is a relatively new phenomenon in our culture. The seventies and eighties were a period of extreme focus not on interpersonal qualities such as emotional vulnerability, transpersonal union, and sexual intimacy but instead on more self-centered qualities such as personal mental development, physical prowess, and material success. Popular books such as *Looking Out for Number One*, *The Uncommitted*, *Single Life*, and *The Culture of Narcissism* documented our general contraction away from the risks and challenges of heartfelt emotional bonding with another person, sexually or otherwise. Individual strengths and achievements were held in high regard, while commitment and anything having to do with vulnerable romantic feelings tended to be regarded as signs of weakness. As Wanda Urbanska stated in *The Singular Generation*, "either through mistrust of love, of intercourse, of members of the opposite sex or even members of the same sex, many people in the eighties recoiled from sexuality, from intimacy, and in some cases even from friendship, whittling their emotional needs down to almost nothing in the process."

Susan and Tom, like so many couples, didn't go to such extremes. Instead, they tried to burn their life candles at both ends. They went strongly into their own individual careers, and kept on top of their separate needs and interests, while also trying to keep a relationship alive. But from the beginning, they set their marriage up to run like a business partnership, not a vulnerable heartfelt commitment. They both thought it was smart to maintain a sense of complete independence, so that they could pull out of the relationship if anything went wrong, just as they would protect their bases in a business deal.

Unfortunately, however, the very traits that made them successful in their business careers were exactly the traits that undermined their ability to achieve a deep sense of spiritual union in their marriage relationship. As businesspeople, they'd had to develop a tough, untrusting, competitive edge to their personalities, never opening themselves vulnerably to possible attack from outside. In their personal relationship, though, this inability to trust, to relinquish control, to risk the loss of personal limits undermined their ability to make contact with each other on spiritual dimensions.

Thus they found themselves with full pocketbooks but, at the same time, a terrible sense of emptiness in their hearts. And like so many other couples, they felt there was no escape from their predicament. They weren't satisfied with their love life, but at the same time they feared separating from each other and losing even the faulted intimacy onto which they were tenuously holding.

Dr. Toni Grant in *Being a Woman* summarized fairly

accurately the emotions that Susan was feeling, the feminine side of the last decade, with the following statement: "Today's woman is an imitation man, at war with actual men, confused and unsettled by it. Many a modern woman is now desperate to rediscover that which she has lost—call it femininity, the power of relatedness, or what you will."

Such feelings were dominant in the heart of Susan when she initiated the spontaneous conversation that soon took over the group meeting. Almost immediately when she was done, several of the men in the group spoke up, admitting that their masculine experience in relationships had been just as difficult and lonely as hers.

Luckily for all of us, time does march on, the eighties are over, and fresh winds are blowing in our culture that offer new hope to people like Susan and Thomas. Just five years ago, if I had offered a sexual-intimacy group in my community, almost no one would have attended. Now courses such as mine have waiting lists and are proliferating throughout the country. As Wanda Urbanska has pointed out, "there is a profound new yearning for the closeness, intimacy, and security that wedlock is supposed to offer."

And this is where the spiritual dimension comes in. The true saving grace of humanity lies not in its ability to manipulate the environment for egocentric aggrandizement. The saving grace of the human community lies in its potential to break beyond the isolation of solitary existence, and to share in the power of love that makes true community possible. Jesus was stating one of the ultimate truths when He pointed out that it is futile to gain the world in material success and power if we lose our souls in the process.

This is one of the major lessons to be learned from the selfish sufferings of the eighties—that life means nothing if we aren't able to share our intimate feelings with someone we love. There is nothing more painful emotionally than being unable to open up and merge with our sexual partner. And there is nothing more beautiful than the awakening of our ability to break beyond ego barriers and become of one spirit with our most intimate friend.

Seven Dimensions to Sexual Fulfillment

The pressing question of the nineties is this: How in reality can we learn to access deeper levels of spiritual union with our sexual partner? What are the actual psychological steps that lead to the awakening of mystic intimacy in a relationship?

My colleagues and I have been exploring these vital questions both in our private therapy practices and marriage-counseling work, and also in more formal academic research, for quite some time now. Many of the answers have been unearthed. Only recently, however, has it been possible to gain a broad enough overview to outline a concise, practical program for encouraging spiritual intimacy in sexual love.

There are upon close examination, as I mentioned before, seven primary stages that lead to spiritual union between lovers. Let me introduce you to each of these stages briefly here in the introduction, and then we will delve individually into each stage with each new chapter. Allow yourself, as you begin reading about each of these dimensions of spiritual sexuality, to begin the vital process of evaluating your own present intimacy situation in light of what you are reading.

Healing Old Heartbreaks

From your very early years of life, you have been involved in a wide variety of intimate relationships. At the beginning of a program such as this, it is essential to look back over your complete history of heart contacts so you can learn to resolve any lingering heartbreaks that might impede your ability to surrender your heart and soul to your present relationship.

For instance, it is very important to reflect on your early relationship with your mother in terms of intimacy to see whether you're still somehow bogged down in this primal relationship in ways that inhibit present-moment merging with your sexual partner. Likewise with your father—were you able to make deep heart contact with him, or was he somehow unavailable for intimate relating?

Were there also other people in your childhood who deeply influenced your understanding of true intimacy in a friendship, who opened their hearts to you and taught you how to love on deep levels of affection and trust? Almost certainly, you had extremely close friends when you were a youngster, bosom buddies with whom you shared the depths of your emerging soul.

Then came puberty, that great rush of sexual awakening in your heart as well as in your genitals. You fell in love, and you had your heart broken, probably a number of times, before you escaped from your teens.

The psychological reality is that only when we have healed all our old heart wounds, sexual or otherwise, are we in position to surrender to the depths of sexual abandon with our present lover. So we will need to devote serious attention to your personal heartbreak status, employing effective techniques for resolving lingering emotional contractions.

Achieving Intimacy Without Drugs

Almost all of us are quite bashful when it comes to initiating sexual intimacy with a new lover. Anything that helps us push through our shyness and inhibitions seems to be a blessing in enabling us to reach out for sexual contact with someone we love or want to get to know more intimately.

For better or for worse, a great many people in our present society push through their inhibitions by using such things as wine, beer, or other alcoholic drinks to help bolster their nerve and sense of sexual abandon. Once a relationship starts off on such a drug-aided footing, it is often quite hard to put aside the alcohol or whatever when making love. Such drugs as marijuana and cocaine, and various sophisticated stimulants that are available either legally or otherwise, very often play a major role in determining the level of intimacy achieved in a sexual relationship.

It is no secret that we are living through a historical period of extreme drug use in our culture. Casual use of a wide variety of drugs, both legal and illegal, is considered almost normal and is even encouraged in many social groups. However, the stark reality is that all drugs distort and disturb our ability to relate at deep spiritual levels of intimacy. Perhaps using drugs reduces our inhibitions and enables us to act out our passions more freely. Ultimately, drugs are an enemy to heart contact, however, because they maintain an avoidance of the raw emotional encounter that is the foundation of an intimate relationship.

This book does not go to the extreme of preaching total abstinence from alcohol or other drugs when making love. Many people report that sometimes in certain ways, alcohol and marijuana, for instance, do add worthwhile dimensions to their sexual relationship. From a spiritual point of view, though, it is very important to learn to risk sexual vulnerability without being under the influence of any drugs at all, so that you establish the foundation of your intimate heart contact outside the haze of any chemical influence.

How do you rate yourself these days regarding your ability to relate to your lover without having to use drugs to reinforce you in your sexual encounters?

Honest Verbal Communication

It's more than obvious that almost all sexual relationships begin through the medium of verbal intercourse, as we let the words of our mouths reach out and make contact with someone we are interested in getting to know better at intimate levels. And the blunt truth is this: If we aren't able to be honest in what we communicate verbally to someone, if our words don't convey our deeper feelings and intentions, then we will have a difficult time being honest with this person when we get down to intimate skin-to-skin levels of relating.

It is so easy to hide our true selves behind a fancy verbal facade that makes us appear more suave and sophisticated, more centered and casual than we actually are at the moment. On the other hand, however, we all hate to sound phony. Our challenge is to learn to throw off our shallow conversational habits so that we can truly speak from the heart to the one we love.

Risking Visual Intercourse

The intimate dimension of relating that we do with our eyes—called visual intercourse in psychological jargon—is often overlooked when discussing sexual fulfillment. As we all know from experience, however, sexual relating is very intensely caught up in those hot, furtive glances and long, overwhelming moments of eye contact that seem to punctuate and define a deepening relationship.

Unfortunately, many of us learned while growing up to avoid using eye contact as a vehicle for intimate exposure and communication. Instead, we habitually protect ourselves from letting anyone look so deeply into our eyes that they see into our very souls, even though without this dimension of sexual relating, true spiritual intimacy simply isn't possible.

Are you someone who habitually looks away from intense visual intercourse? And if so, would you like to begin to expand your ability to enter into the truly mystic experience of seeing and being seen instantly and to the core of your being?

Skin-to-Skin Intimacy

A sexual involvement always leads inexorably to the moment when clothes drop away and all is laid bare to our lover, even our most secret and sensual parts. The movement toward sexual union requires a steady shifting from conversation and social games to more intimate nonverbal behavior. We must be ready to let go of thoughts, let go of anticipations, let go of the future entirely if we are able to enter into the magic of the eternal present moment where spiritual relating actually happens.

The large majority of us have extreme difficulty in silencing our thinking minds, however. Instead, we are chronically held prisoner by the flow of thoughts that continue to distract our attention from sensual encounter and the merging of our soul with that of our beloved.

If this is a difficulty in your own lovemaking, perhaps the time has come to confront your mental habits, to evaluate your skin-to-skin behavior, and to learn how to move beyond your thinking mind and into the expanded state of spiritual union and sexual merging.

Transcending Fantasy Games

Of equal importance is the challenge of breaking free from habitual fantasy games that tend to grip our minds and keep us from experiencing a direct encounter with our lover. So many of us are, in fact, addicts to sexual fantasy. Right when we should be totally involved in the perceptual reality of the present moment with our lover, we find ourselves being pulled off into old internal fantasy games that stimulate us through masturbatory channels but shut us off from direct sensory and mystic contact with the person with whom we are making love.

Fantasizing while having sexual intercourse was lauded in the seventies and eighties as a great way to heighten a sexual experience. It certainly does increase masturbatory stimulation. If you want to encounter your lover at spiritual levels of true union, however, you must put aside all fantasies, just as you put aside drugs and compulsive thinking and talking, so that your individual ego can melt into a new sense of oneness with your lover.

Ultimate Sexual Transformation

Much has been said regarding the orgasm experience in recent decades. We have established, for instance, that many women fake orgasms to make their partner feel potent. We have also established that many men ejaculate without reaching a deeper triggering of their male orgasm experience. Scientists can speak for hours on end concerning the anatomy and stimulus-response paradigms of the orgasm. But what is the true nature of the orgasm experience from a spiritual point of view?

Without doubt, the extended orgasm experience offers a truly remarkable organic opportunity for breaking temporarily free of our isolated ego identities, and expanding our awareness so that we exist momentarily in union with the person with whom we are having intercourse. The orgasm is in fact nature's way of transporting us into transcendent states of consciousness, if only for a brief period of time. In this amazing way, we have built into our human systems direct access to spiritual bliss.

Many of us, however, identify so intensely with our isolated sense of individuality that we are afraid to let go and be transported by an orgasm into greater realms of being, perhaps even into a momentary state of total union with the universe and beyond—with God or whatever name we choose to call the ultimate spiritual reality.

This book is not fixated upon the physiological orgasm

as the only point in lovemaking where transcendence is attained. In fact, we will explore an expanded definition of orgasm that liberates us from the somewhat crass mutual-masturbation approach to orgasm that has been popular recently. We will see how true orgasm is a whole-body experience, wherein not just the genitals but the entire mystic body is transported into bliss during sexual climax.

The Growth Process in Action

I have just discussed with you in quite rapid succession seven very major points regarding how you relate with your lover. Please don't think I am asking you to judge yourself on these seven dimensions. We are simply beginning the process whereby you reflect upon each of these seven dimensions of sexual intimacy at more and more insightful levels, and, where needed, apply the pragmatic techniques you will be learning in the following chapters for expanding your capacity for spiritual intercourse with your sexual partner.

In this light, one of the most important things we have learned about personal growth and spiritual fulfillment is that in order to advance into new realms of being, we must first of all accept ourselves as perfectly okay just the way we are right now. Rather than judging ourselves as presently inadequate, we need to open our hearts to ourselves even with all our seeming problems and inhibitions. We also need to come to perceive our lover in the same acceptant light.

At first this might seem to be a contradiction. If we accept ourselves as okay just as we are, won't we lose the impetus for pushing ahead? If we relax and love ourselves without judgment, won't we remain stuck in our obvious blocks and contractions?

Joel Kramer, in his classic spiritual-reflection manual entitled *The Passionate Mind*, has made the following key point regarding personal evolution into deeper levels of interaction: "It is not the desire to evolve that brings evolution, but rather the total seeing of oneself." We cannot in fact force ourselves to change deep down. We cannot change our past, for instance. And a great deal of our mental and emotional wiring is of such a genetic nature that we cannot hope to rewire it. We will always be who we are.

However, we can actively learn to look honestly and passionately at what we have done in the past, and how we are behaving in the present moment. We can learn to pause in our hectic, often manic, sometimes depressive fixations on things other than our own presence, and breathe into our potent encounters with our own selves. Especially to achieve the goals set forth in this book, we must diligently look at how we have related with lovers both long gone and with our lover perhaps just last night.

This seemingly simple mental process of passionately observing ourselves in action both in the past and in the present moment is the one true vehicle for generating spontaneous growth of our personality. A very fine contemporary spiritual teacher named Krishnamurti, whom I had the blessing to study with before his death, made this "flame of attention" to our own thoughts, memories, and perceptions the center point of his entire philosophical and spiritual vision of life.

What we are doing in this book is applying this level of potent spiritual techniques to the actual everyday act of sexual intercourse. By expanding our awareness of the seven vital dimensions of spiritual and sexual communion, we will spontaneously awaken deep personal growth inside us in the present moment.

As we will see in later chapters, the ultimate goal is to maintain this deep awareness right in the midst of sexual passion while making love. Suddenly, when we move into more mystic states of mind, our earthly passions take on a transformed energy as we move effortlessly into a breathtaking new dimension of pure mystic experience.

Within the Zen meditative tradition of Japan is to be found the perfect description of the most important lesson regarding how to make love. The Zen masters state simply that there is "nowhere to go and nothing to do" in order to attain union with the divine. Pushing for orgasm, struggling with sex postures, playing psychological games with ourselves and our sexual partners—such efforts only muddy the mystic waters.

We must learn instead the effortless path in which we simply become more aware of the totality of who we are, more sensitive to our spontaneous perceptions and desires, more open to our divine nature as it already exists, perfect and fulfilled in the present moment. Then the grace of spiritual bliss can come flooding into our bodies, into our emotions, into our minds and our souls, transforming our lover's coupling into infinite realization and pleasure.

The bottom line on spiritual intimacy is that it is a quality of relating that simply cannot be forced into existence. It comes as a blessing, as an effortless magical experience. All we can do is learn to clear our minds of the obstacles that habitually block intimate contact. Then we can just relax in a deep but also playful mood with our lover, and consciously open ourselves to the beneficent inflow of the holy spirit of sexual love.

With this in mind, I encourage you from the beginning

to take a deep breath, accept that you are okay just as you are right now, and relax as you try to see yourself more clearly, more honestly, more compassionately. This book will serve as a gentle and regular reminder of important directions on which to focus your attention. You have only to discipline yourself to look deeply in the seven directions we reviewed a moment ago and will explore in greater depth later on. And all you are risking in final analysis is a direct spiritual encounter with yourself—and in extension with your sexual partner, and the universe beyond.

Certainly there are times when we must struggle to grow through old contractions and inhibitions. Growth always includes its painful and scary moments. Ultimately, however, love flourishes when we are at peace, when we are content with ourselves, when we are able to loosen up and play around joyfully with our lover.

Men and Women Together

Very often it is the woman in a sexual relationship who first seeks out help in learning to expand her level of heart contact with her lover. This was the case with Susan, for instance. It is a serious injustice to men to judge them as insensitive to their own hungers for deep intimate contact, however.

Thus I wasn't so very surprised, at the second meeting of my sexual-intimacy group, to see Susan walk into the room accompanied by a tall young man named Thomas. Coming from his background, it was a great step he made in venturing into such an emotionally risky situation in order to explore his potential for achieving intimate union with his partner. In fact, though, it was Thomas more than many of the others who very often spoke up in the group to share his changing emotions and reflections. "I remember now how Susan wanted sometimes just to relax with me and be intimate a bit before we would take off in opposite directions for work," he mentioned during the fifth meeting of the group. "But from the time I woke up, I was always instantly in business gear, I completely ignored her feelings. Now that I see how I used to be, things are changing, but still most of the time my head automatically goes into work gear if she doesn't point it out to me."

It's always a great pleasure to see couples coming alive to each other's presence and desires. Usually the stereotype of the awakening couple is of two young lovers discovering each other. In reality, however, it is a great mistake to assume that just the younger generation is wanting to be victorious in the struggle to achieve true intimacy. A great many people over forty-five are also openly fed up with the inhibitions placed upon their shoulders by their strict upbringing, and are ready to stand up and insist on their birthright of deep, intimate contact both sexual and otherwise. My spiritual-sexuality courses are in fact populated quite equally with younger folks, middle-aged, and senior-citizen participants.

Whatever our age, background, or social status, we all share the primal need for emotional bonding, for sexual surrender, for spiritual transcendence of our tiny little bubbles of self-importance and solitude. It is therefore no accident or surprise that sexual intimacy and spiritual intercourse are among the key buzzwords of the nineties. As one psychologist put it several years ago, "my generation still finds the myth of everlasting marriage far more attractive than the singular reality. Indeed, everlasting marriage is the unfulfilled wish-fantasy of the eighties."

My deep-felt intent in writing this book is to enable the

wish fantasy of the eighties to become the fulfilled reality of the nineties. Long-term intimate sexual relationships are the essential foundation of human civilization. We all need to devote our concerted attention and energy to preserving and expanding the presence of spiritual sexuality in our lives.

THE "SPIRITUAL INTIMACY" QUESTIONNAIRE

Each of us has our own unique set of desires and habits when it comes to making love. There are times when having sex is just that—a simple physical discharge of bodily tensions following a temporary period of sensual pleasure. Sometimes, however, sexual love suddenly becomes transformed into a remarkable spiritual encounter with the divine as we discover the deeper mystic realms of sexual relating.

As a beginning exploration of your own present sexual-intimacy situation in life, notice what thoughts and feelings arise spontaneously as you contemplate each of the following questions, first for yourself, and then, if you wish, for your lover, as well.

1. Do you often feel the desire for deeper sexual intimacy with your lover or marriage partner?
2. Do you feel free to talk with your sexual partner about your more intimate emotional feelings?
3. Can you easily surrender to the wild, spontaneous rush of sexual abandon that leads to mystic orgasm?
4. Do you receive enough tender love and affection in your romantic life to satisfy your heart?
5. Are you able to open up and share your deep sexual secrets with your lover/mate?

6. How often in your present life do you find yourself feeling lonely?

7. Can you let go of your separate sense of self while making love, and surrender to the spiritual power of total orgasm?

8. Do you often gaze into your lover's eyes and experience the tremulous melting passion of visual intercourse?

9. When making love, can you readily let go of thoughts and fantasies so that you tune into the present-moment intensity of spiritual levels of intercourse?

10. Does your lover allow you to look deeply into his or her secret inner realms of mystic presence?

11. Would you say that you still carry guilt feelings inside you related to some of your sexual desires and activities?

12. Do you sometimes feel painfully anxious right in the middle of lovemaking?

13. Do you often use drugs of one kind or another to push you into wild abandon and uninhibited sexual passion?

14. Are you free occasionally to express aggressive emotions with your sexual partner?

15. Would you say there is a feeling of mutual respect and equality in your sexual relationship?

16. Do you and your partner share the desire to explore realms of spiritual awakening through your sexual relating?

17. Do you sometimes feel right on the edge of surrendering to a deeper mystic reality when making love?

18. Were you brought up to see sex and spirit as opposites, or did your parents include sexuality as a spiritual experience?

19. When making love, do you and your sexual partner

relax and let passion come of itself, or do you often push for release?

20. Do you feel free of the wounds and influence of old romantic relationships, or are you still somehow hung up in the past?

21. How often do you feel the inflow of a spiritual energy and presence into your body and soul while making love?

22. Have you already shared with your lover the feeling of total merging and spiritual oneness, or is this ultimate experience still in your future?

23. After making love, do you drift apart immediately or linger in each other's arms in the ecstasy of vibrant heart contact?

24. Would you say that you are ready for a radical new phase of spiritual discovery in your sexual relationship?

1

Letting Old Heartbreaks Heal

Roger's childhood, like that of too many others, was a rugged one. He grew up in a home where his father and mother were often at odds with each other. When he was ten, his mom ran off with another man for three months before returning to her family. Roger never quite trusted her after that; he felt heartbroken and wouldn't open up to her again. Now as an adult, Roger has repeatedly exhibited the romantic pattern of venturing just so far into a sexual relationship, then breaking off the commitment, afraid deep down that if he allows himself to bond with a woman in deep union, he might ultimately be abandoned as he felt his mother abandoned him. Thus his past holds him a prisoner in the present moment.

Roger was the kind of person who would never even think of walking into an intimacy group as Thomas did. He was guarded in his expression of his emotions, and avoided groups where he had to contribute anything. But he happened to work with a man who was a client of mine. They talked a lot on the job, and finally, at the tail end of yet another failed romance, he phoned me one afternoon and asked to come by for a chat.

His heart wound proved to be more severe than most, and it took quite some time for him to work through his childhood trauma to where he could trust and love a woman with his whole heart. Aside from the level of intensity, however, his basic problem was a universal one—he had once surrendered himself to a total sense of trust and love in a deep heart relationship, had been let down and plunged into a terrible feeling of abandonment, and was afraid to experience that level of heartbreak again.

"I'm damned if I do and damned if I don't," he told me during our initial conversation. "It's hell getting involved with someone, really needing her, and being afraid she'll dump me. But it's even worse hell living alone. Ever since I was ten, I've felt I've been living alone, and I can't stand it. I understand what my mother was going through. I try to forgive her. But somehow I'm still stuck back in the past; I can't shake free of it."

Each and every one of us has had our heart broken at least once in our lives, perhaps by our mother or father, perhaps by a close childhood friend, quite probably by at least one lover. Entering into deep bonded relationships and then having to end such relationships for one reason or another is an integral part of a full, healthy life. Our ongoing challenge is to recover from these old heartbreaks so that we can open up and love again. Otherwise, we continue to carry around in our hearts the aching pain of abandonment and rejection. In such a contracted emotional state, we are unable to live and love fully in the present moment, which is where spiritual ecstasy is realistically to be found.

Many people such as Roger continue to feel wounded even decades after they have had their hearts broken. Instead of going through the essential mourning and acceptance process that allows a heart to heal, they contract and often even deny what has happened to them, thus blocking the healing process that naturally occurs if we let ourselves feel the pain and grow through it.

In this chapter, we're going to explore both the bonding process that forges a friendship between two people and the psychological process that enables us to recover and move on to a new love relationship after an intimate bonding is broken. This first phase of dealing with past intimacies is absolutely essential in learning to awaken a deeper sense of trust and intimacy in present sexual involvements.

However, I am not a depressive therapist looking always for the negative, and forcing people to wallow endlessly in painful memories. This process of looking back to assess and reexperience earlier intimate relationships can be primarily a joyous adventure when approached in an acceptant and compassionate way.

In your own past, for instance, each time you entered into a new love relationship of any kind whatsoever, you most certainly felt a remarkably beautiful feeling as you opened your heart to a new person, and gained a new level of intimacy. It is extremely important to recover and move beyond the contractions of old emotional wounds so that you can regain in your heart all the priceless beautiful feelings you shared with past friends and lovers. You have a vast treasure of intimate memories from your past that should serve as the foundation for your present ecstatic unions. Instead of each new love canceling out the last love, previous intimacies should resonate with and amplify a new relationship's intensity.

In the various sections of this chapter, we are going to look deeply into the primary intimacies and friendships you had as a child and young adult, so you can actively reap the harvest of past involvements of the heart while also healing any old wounds that are holding you back from present emotional and spiritual surrender.

We will begin with your relationship with your mother, that primal involvement that taught you so much about love, and that also sometimes stands in the way of mature sexual surrender.

Mothers Imperfect

Therapists are famous for mother-bashing sprees that dump all blame for a person's heart problems onto his or her mother and her inadequacies in performing the mothering role. What therapists usually fail to mention is that the mothering role in itself is actually an impossible one to do perfectly. The demands of a child are beyond the capacity of any one woman to meet fully.

For instance, each of us instinctively expected our mother to be there for us all the time with total love and acceptance. At the same time, we were busy demanding that she let go of us so we could carry on with our independent lives. Furthermore, as young children, we expected our mothers to understand our every inner feeling and need, to anticipate our desires, to know what was going on inside our own minds and instantly respond to our buried emotions.

No mother can fulfill this impossible challenge. Thus, as

little kids, we all felt let down many times when we found ourselves out in the emotional cold, not understood adequately to satisfy our inner needs fully. We also felt hurt each time she pushed us further away from her so that we could become more independent, and she could have a bit of the separate peace she hungered for in her own personal life.

In spite of these inevitably painful dimensions to the mother-child relationship, most of us also experienced a primal heartfelt emotional bonding with our mothers or mother figures, a special sense of oneness that later served as the foundation for all future heart encounters in our lives. Joseph Chilton Pearce, one of the most advanced teachers and writers in our culture regarding child development, sexual relating, and spiritual fulfillment, has described in his recent book *Magical Child Matures* the dynamics of this vital bonding process between mother and child.

For instance, while still in the womb, we experienced a sense of total blissful unity with our mother. She was the universe for us until we were born; she was the great goddess who provided us not only with all our physical needs but who also allowed us to live within a perfect boundless infinity of being. This womb experience formed the experiential basis for all our later mystic searchings and realizations. Because we once lived through this seemingly infinite period of oneness with another human being, with another body in which we were subhumed, we all have the natural desire to enter again into this womblike state of pure bliss—and this is exactly what happens on certain levels while making love.

During intercourse, a man can quite physically place himself right back where he started in the womb. A woman has a different sexual experience in this regard. If you are a woman, as you matured, you became aware of the presence of your own womb deep within you. During intercourse, when your mind finally lets go of all head trips and turns its total attention to your sexual regions, you find yourself coming alive again with feelings that resonate with your own womb experiences before you were born.

When as adults we remain in conflict with our mothers, when we have our hearts closed to them because in some way we feel they rejected us, even abandoned us, then we find ourselves unable to make deep contact with our own womb experience during intercourse. Alexander Lowen made the point clearly in his book *Love and Orgasm* that such an emotional blockage directly inhibits the whole-body orgasm experience.

Therefore, regardless of how we were treated by our mothers while growing up, it is essential to keep our hearts open to the womb from which we came, and in extension to accept and forgive our mothers on all fronts. Later in this chapter, I will speak further about this process of letting go of negative feelings toward one's parents.

For now, let me give you some free time at this point so that you can put the book aside after reading this paragraph and let your mind reflect a bit regarding your present sense of connectedness with your beginnings in the womb. See if you can imagine yourself floating in perpetual bliss inside your mother's womb, immersed in a pervading sense of unity with the universe, hearing your mother's heartbeat along with your own, feeling no sense of separation from her at all.

Consider Thy Father

In many mammalian species, the father simply is not present at all in the life of a child. The mother does the entire job of raising the offspring. In the land of the mythical Amazon women, the same situation was supposed to have existed, where men were needed only for insemination of the mighty and otherwise self-sufficient women.

Sometimes this is how life happens for children in our own culture as well. Even when the father is present in the house and provides the material well-being for the family, he can remain emotionally detached, not offering the children the opportunity to bond with him in an intimate heart relationship.

In other families just the opposite can happen—the father can play an equal role to the mother in the development of a child's ability to enter into intimate levels of friendship. In the early months there is obviously a natural fixation on the mother, since she is the source of primary nourishment, and since the baby has come out of her womb and is therefore already bonded with her. But after that, the openness of the father's heart to the child determines the level of bonding that will occur between them.

We live in a society where certain roles are usually assigned to the father, while others are assigned to the mother, and these roles strongly influence the ways in which we develop our relationships with our fathers. For instance, traditionally God has been seen as a man, as a powerful, dominating male presence coming down from His throne on high, enforcing His laws with a swift and often severe sword. Fathers who identify with this paternal-dominance pattern will tend to keep themselves separate from their children, afraid to risk what would happen if they let their guard down and became equals with the rest of the family, relating in vulnerable, gentle, unjudging ways.

Fathers are without doubt different from mothers, and little children are extremely conscious of these differences. There is first of all the phallic presence of a man in the house, and all that this phallus represents. A little boy will usually feel a shared physical sense of masculinity with his father. For a little girl, there is the sense of a primal difference between her and Daddy. This difference becomes a crucial issue later on as the girl develops her own sense of sexual identity.

One of the primary acts of a father in a household is the usually regular occurrence of sexual activity between this giant of a phallic monster and the child's precious Mommy. It goes without saying that we learn about sex first from our parents, either through their open expression of their sexual desire for each other or through their inhibitions regarding their sexuality.

Traditionally in our culture, parents have tended to hide their sexual intimacies from their children, acting as if there was something frightening or even wrong in revealing their sexual feelings in the presence of their youngsters. Many children grow up without ever seeing their father's penis or their mother's breasts, since very often parents are embarrassed to be naked with their children. When these parental inhibitions exist, children grow up with a basic fear and even an inherited sense of disgust related to sexual organs and lustful passions.

For girls more than for boys, there is also the lurking dimension of father-daughter sexual involvement that can pollute a sincere sense of intimacy between father and child. As I have found over and over again with male clients in my therapy work, even fathers who would never be incestuous toward their daughters find themselves inhibiting their flow of loving warmth and affection toward their young daughters for fear that others might suspect them of incestuous desires. The daughter thus feels rejected by her father for no seeming reason at all.

As an example, a client of mine expressed her childhood feelings toward her father with the following painful remembrance: "I had no idea what was happening, but when I went through puberty and my body filled out and I started getting all sorts of romantic feelings inside me, my dad seemed to change his relationship with me completely. Instead of giving me a hug and a kiss in the mornings like he used to, he started just firing mean glares at me, as if I'd done something wrong. It broke my heart; it really hurt me so deeply that I just started to run wild, and by the time I was fifteen, I was pregnant and had to have an abortion, and that just made Dad hate me more. Now I can look back and see that he was probably confused and afraid of my budding sexuality, but when it was happening, I just thought he didn't like me anymore, that he was disgusted by my breasts and everything."

Thus fathers can teach us how to love, yet can equally teach us how to draw away from love. Eva Pierrakos, one of the truly deep teachers of the heart path in sexual relating, spoke often in her book *The Pathwork of Self-Transformation* of the necessity to look back and remember clearly the reality of our feelings toward our fathers as well as our mothers. She made the point that "it is possible to be both happy and unhappy" in our childhood relationships with our fathers, and that "we can only forgive and let go if we recognize our deeply hidden hurts and resentments" toward our parents that continue to pollute our present relationships.

Let me give you time once again to pause and put the book aside after reading this paragraph in order to reflect upon your childhood involvement with your father. Did you hunger for more warmth and affection, more attention and understanding than he gave to you, or were you truly satisfied heartwise in your involvement with him? Furthermore, have you accepted and forgiven him where he might have been inadequate, or are you still bearing him a grudge deep inside you that needs to be resolved? Relax and breathe into whatever feelings come to you as you turn your attention back to your interactions with your father in your family home.

Childhood Best Friends

No matter how much love and affection a child receives at home, there is still an ingrained impetus in each youngster to establish friendships outside the family circle with boys and girls one's own age. Almost every child does find someone in school or elsewhere in the community with whom to be intimate friends. This is a vital dimension to growing up. At the same time, however, these early heart bondings, which are often beautifully pure and of a truly spiritual nature, almost always come to an end.

Most adults with whom I have explored this question no longer know of the whereabouts and well-being of their early childhood friends. The magic of the friendship remains as a vague memory of genuine trust and love, but at some point the magic went away, the friendship died, and life went on. "I remember being crushed when Teresa started hanging out with a new girlfriend and didn't want to be close with me anymore," a friend of mine recalled recently when we talked over this topic. "My mother tried to help me through the heartbreak, but there was nothing anybody could do. I suffered for weeks. I guess I was about eight years old then. If I'd known what suicide was, I might have even contemplated ending my life, the depression was so intense that first time, worse than ever it would be with later relationships. But then I met this other girl and we teamed up and suddenly life was bright again. I could breathe, I had a new friend."

It is a remarkable and yet seldom-discussed observation among therapists I know that a great many adults are going through their entire lives trying in vain to establish new friendships like the priceless early ones they knew in child-hood. One of my colleagues has even gone so far as to state that "one of the primary reasons couples break up is that the present relationship lacks the intensity, the intimacy, the deep bonding that once existed in a childhood friendship. Even though we can never regain that quality of intimacy that we knew as children, many of us still waste our lives seeking after it. This must be one of the great pities of human interaction."

I partly agree with her. We do hunger for the lost inno-cence and potency of childhood friendships, and the sad truth is that we have gone through so many transformations as we moved into maturity that we will never again be able to experience certain of the mythic realms of childhood friendship. Therefore, we have no choice but to let go of this buried agenda, this underground hungering for some-thing we knew in the past, if we are to reap the blessings that are available to us in our present level of maturity.

At the same time, it is important to note, especially in a book such as this, that our present "feel" for what it means to be best friends with someone was in fact primarily developed through those early friendships of our childhood. Even though we can't duplicate such intense feelings as we experi-enced early in our life, we certainly can aim to achieve the adult equivalent.

One of the premises of this book is that it is impossible to open ourselves to spiritual surrender in a mature sexual relationship unless there also exists a deep level of platonic friendship with our lover, where we feel that same depth of trust and acceptance that we felt for our special friends when we were young. In therapy, I very often have clients do exactly what I am suggesting to you—that you reclaim the feeling in your heart that you had for your best friends as a child, so that this feeling can come alive again in your present relationship, transformed of course by the years that have gone by but, in essence, of similar quality.

A good friend of mine, whom I have known for twenty-some years now, ever since college, has gone through three marriages and perhaps a dozen deep sexual involvements after leaving her childhood home. We got together a few days ago when she flew into town, and talked late into the night. She told me with bright, satisfied eyes that she has been in her present marriage for six years now, having finally found the man for whom she was looking. "It was well worth all the pain and the searching," she told me. "Don is the first man I've been with sexually whom I can also be best friends with, whom I can just relax with like I used to relax with my girlfriend when I was a kid. That's what I was missing before, and I simply couldn't go through my life without it."

Sexual vulnerability requires this level of friendship if one is to open into mystic realms of interaction during love-making. The reason for this requirement is that we must become totally defenseless at the point of true spiritual orgasm. If there isn't deep trust and friendship in a sexual relationship, your deeper spirit simply will not risk the vulnerability needed for mystic merging of your soul with that of another person. And afterward, you will feel depressed rather than blissful, because you approached the great mystery of creation, the ultimate vastness of spiritual love, and yet were unable to trust enough to break on through to the other side.

So I encourage you now, and in the days and weeks to come, to look back regularly to remember the deep friendships you had when you were growing up. Through reliving your childhood experiences of intimate friendship, you will reawaken the feeling in your heart that you felt for your childhood intimates, and actively bring this power of trust and affection into your present relationship.

Reliving Your Childhood

Let me give you a key self-help therapeutic vehicle for accessing such memories, since I can't be with you to guide you personally through the process. You can do this readily whenever you have perhaps five to ten minutes of peace and relative quiet. Since this crucial beginning chapter is all about reliving your earlier phases of life and reaping the great rewards from such memory expeditions, I hope you take time to delve deeply into each of the memory sessions I am suggesting. The payoff in the present moment with your lover will be quite remarkable.

Here is the basic "memory expedition" process to memorize and then practice regularly in the days and weeks to come.

Either sit or lie comfortably . . . tune into your breathing as each new breath comes and goes . . . stretch and feel your whole body alive here in the present moment . . . allow your eyes to close when they want to . . . feel the air rushing in and out your nose as you breathe . . . let thoughts fall away

. . . be aware of the movement in your chest and belly with each new breath . . . and now in this relaxed, open state, let your mind turn in the general direction of the person or theme in your past you want to remember . . . stay aware of your breathing as memories begin to come effortlessly to you . . . stay aware of your emotions . . . and let the memories take you where they will.

This basic "soft hypnosis" technique will quickly transport you into deep recall of the person or theme you are holding in mind when you go through the simple focusing process. Each time you go on such a "memory expedition," you will find that you can go deeper and deeper into reliving moments in your past. And this intense remembering will serve as a powerful stimulus for awakening seemingly lost feelings inside your heart, and for generating a spontaneous healing experience.

Of course, with your mother, your father, and your childhood friends, there will come painful memories as well as blissful ones. The key to emotional healing is to let yourself experience passionately the emotions that accompanied important events in your past. Healing takes place right at the point where you remember a buried experience, feel the accompanying emotions intensely, and accept exactly what did happen to you. Then you can forgive, let go of the past, and come more fully into the present moment. As Eva Pierrakos has put it, "by experiencing all these emotions from the past, you will leave your childhood truly behind, and start new inner behavior patterns that will be infinitely more constructive and rewarding."

To bring our focus of attention back to the present theme of this section—that of reliving the power and depth of early childhood friendships—see what experience comes to you if you put the book aside after finishing this paragraph and turn your loving attention to a long-gone but very

important intimacy you shared with a true friend from childhood days.

Teachers Along the Heart Path

The next almost-universal occurrence in our evolution toward mature sexual relating is the phenomenon usually re-
ferred to as "puppy love." Right when puberty begins first
to awaken wild new passions inside a youngster, there is the
tendency to fall in love in a quasisexual way with an older
person, often a teacher in school. This first flush of passion
is extremely important to later development, and emerges
out of a deep process of ego development in adolescence.
Suddenly, seemingly overnight, a child wakes up to a new
feeling, a new hunger, which is felt as both a sexual and a
spiritual passion in the body and mind.

In *Magical Child Matures*, Joseph Chilton Pearce described how the first twelve or so years of a child's life are
focused mostly on biologically dictated development, as the
child's body manifests the preprogrammed blueprints that
come with genetic inheritance. Once this first major phase
of development is completed, what Pearce has called the
"post-biological" development of a human being begins in
earnest—and this development is the progressive realization
of the maturing child that there exists an expansive spiritual
dimension beyond the confines of biological life.

"Whatever we call post-biological identification of ego—
the psyche, the soul, or the spirit," Pearce stated, "the function is the same. I use the term 'spirit' because I like it; but
I refer not to some vapid, vague, insubstantial ethereal body
emanating in a seance, but to the exuberant, explosive cre-

ative power bubbling up from our hearts in adolescence, when we manifest the first inkling of our identities with the creative power bringing our universe into being."

The first flush of sexual awakening in a youngster is as delicate a phenomenon as the proverbial pushing of a fragile blade of grass through the earth and into the air above. Our first experiences of sexual passion, and the responses of people around us to our emerging sexuality, established patterns deep within us that continue to influence us throughout life. So it is extremely important for us to consciously relive and reflect upon our first passionate desires and sexual awakenings that came to us in puberty.

The awakening of a human being's spiritual consciousness does seem to be directly stimulated by the parallel awakening during puberty of sexual consciousness. As mentioned earlier, this is the primary thrust of this book—that our most natural vehicle for spiritual awakening and contact with the divine is through sexual intimacy and intercourse. It is therefore quite essential to look back and remember that period in our pubescent lives when the dawning realization of our creative sexual powers came to us and empowered our discovery of new mystic dimensions to life.

I might mention as an aside that religious devotees who denounce all sexual activity in order to become more spiritual do not in actual practice manage to turn off their sexual juices. Instead, they learn through various meditation techniques to rechannel their sexual energies away from physiological orgasm and into more whole-body bliss. The primal energy being employed is one and the same, as the meditative traditions of Hinduism, Buddhism, and Taoism all openly acknowledge. And in the Roman Catholic monastic tradition, almost always it was right at the first flush of puberty that young boys and girls would choose or be pushed into renouncing earthly sexual desires, and retreat into a monastery to learn to redirect their sexual energies into spiritual manifestations.

For most of us in contemporary society however, there existed no option for avoiding plunging headlong into sexual awakening. In our first wild flush of puppy love, we didn't have any perspective on what was happening inside us. We simply found ourselves possessed by a radical new energy in our bodies, by a mystic new spirit in our souls, and in total innocence we found ourselves fixating this new energy of the heart and genitals toward a particular person, very often a teacher of the opposite sex with whom we found ourselves infatuated at an almost excruciating level of intensity.

"She was the Spanish teacher at the private school I was attending," a client said to me as he lay relaxed in a light trance, reliving his first puppy-love infatuation. "I can see her now standing in front of the class, she's tall, totally beautiful in my eyes, and she instantly makes me feel weak in the stomach when she glances my way. I can barely stand to be in the room with her, the feelings are so intense in my body. It's not a sexual feeling, in that I'm not focused on my balls and penis, I can't quite describe it except to say that my whole body feels just like my penis does sometimes when I'm just ready to come. There's a passion, a hunger, I can hardly breathe. My mind is cloudy, and when she calls on me to conjugate the verb *to carry*, my voice is so weak she shouts at me to speak up. But I can't. Her eyes hold mine for just a split second once I have finished with the conjugation. I can see that she feels something for me too, and my heart suddenly is pumping in my chest so painfully I stand up and ask to be excused to go to the bathroom. Outside, I'm sweating, my body feels like it will explode. I take off running down the corridor of the school, feeling as if I could leap into the air and fly."

For the first time in his life, this particular boy was feeling the ultimate ecstasy and agony of sexual desire, feeling it much more intensely than he would in later romantic affairs, at least until he learned again as an adult how to merge spirit with sex, to become innocent and permeable while making love.

In a later session, this client went on to relive his first ejaculation, which came about four months after his first feelings of puppy love for his teacher. He was in bed at night, innocently playing with himself while dreaming of the teacher, and the heat of passion carried him to that masculine point of no return, where for the first time he felt the explosive male ecstasy of seminal ejaculation.

"I was very religious back then. I remember jumping up and running to the bathroom, knowing that I had somehow done something terribly sinful. I even prayed to God right at that point; I could feel his presence watching me and I prayed that if he would forgive me, I would never do that terrible thing again. But then the very next night, I did do it again."

Thus with boys, the pressure of puppy love is often released through masturbation. As jerking off becomes a secret habit, the genitals quickly gain dominance over the rest of the body as the fixation point for sexual pleasure and release. Boys have no choice in this—they start ejaculating out of physiological pressure, coming in their sleep if they don't ejaculate while awake. Girls, on the other hand, have a more subtle physiology sexually, remaining more in a whole-body, heart-centered experience of sexual passion, often not discovering for months or years their own ability to release their sexual pressures through masturbation.

"It was my girlfriend's father that I fell in love with, when I was just turning twelve, a few months before I started my first period," a close friend told me recently when I asked her in confidence about her first puppy-love experience. "He was a soft, sensual man, very different from my own father. He would glance at me when I came into his house with my girlfriend, and I would feel just blasted away. I could tell from his eyes that he was interested in me sexually. He wasn't the kind of man to take advantage of a virginal girl, but he was usually packing a charge sexually and it would hit me instantly. Several times when I was playing with my girlfriend, we heard him and his wife making love in their bedroom upstairs, and we would giggle but then fall silent, listening, unable to meet each other's eyes. So when he started taking notice of me, I instantly felt he wanted me in bed with him, and the idea set me on fire. I didn't imagine him inside me, I hadn't quite gotten to that point in my fantasies. But I remember waking up late at night sweaty all over from a dream in which he had been chasing me, and then had caught me, and stood over me naked. After that, I sometimes would lie in bed feeling myself and imagining what he might do to me if he got the chance. Those were delicious fantasies. That was when I first realized that some-day sometime some man would be inside me. Sometimes even now I find myself still drifting back to the fantasy of having him as a lover. Amazing how those early fantasies linger."

If we are honest with ourselves and can awaken our pubescent memories sufficiently, each of us has our own secret tales to tell of our very first romantic hungers that were of a genital nature. I have now given you some general notions regarding puppy love. It is time for me to fall silent so that you can pause in your reading, put the book aside if you so choose, and venture into a memory expedition focused on your own first puppy-love experience, perhaps with a teacher in school, perhaps with a fellow student. Take a few minutes now to relax, turn your attention back to your past, and enjoy the rush of emotions that come to you as you relive the passions of your first puppy-love involvement.

Pristine Romance

Our first puppy-love infatuation usually lasts only a short time, a few weeks or months at the most, before being replaced by a new and usually at least slightly more available object of our affections, another human being out there in the world who somehow magically comes to attain the status of our own ideal beloved.

Adults tend to forget just how raw and often abrasive the emotions of those teen years can be. The truth is that early patterns of inhibition and emotional hunger that get established in high school can influence adult life for many decades. Almost always in therapy, there comes the time when it is essential to go back and relive many of the school-day experiences that still haunt a person's psyche, creating unwanted contractions and completely inappropriate emotional reactions in adult life.

"She was a soft beautiful bird of a girl, untouchable, so young she could hardly look in a boy's eyes—and when she did risk visual intimacies, it was always with someone else and not me," another client confessed. "I wanted her so badly, I sometimes would come home after school and walk into my bedroom and hit the door so hard with my fist I would bleed. I was just fifteen, she was the first girl that got to me that way. I would lie in bed and dream of saying things to her, dream that she said things back to me. And sure, I was only normal, I'd dream of doing everything to her. If there's such a thing as ESP, she must have felt herself shot full on a nightly basis for months. Then came the big homecoming prom. I finally got up the nerve to walk up to her and ask her to go with me. She sort of glanced at me casually and said, 'Oh, well, no, I don't think so.' I felt like I'd been stabbed in the chest. It took me months to get over hating her. I think I still hate her. She devastated me."

In contrast to these unrequited passions of love, most of us also managed to find someone to play out the first positive stanzas of romantic bonding with, usually someone about our age, someone bashful too but, like we were, hungry to finally hold someone's hand, to merge with at what now seem purely innocent levels of sexual intimacy but at the time felt like total emotional orgasm.

"I don't quite remember how it started," a friend told me regarding her first boyfriend. "I do remember sitting across from him in English class and suddenly feeling his eyes on me, and glancing his way and finding him looking into my eyes with a hot stare of desire that just melted me. I remember feeling myself pulsing with a soft full liquid sensation, then I would realize I wasn't breathing. . . . Somehow at some point we managed to start up a conversation after class, and we just fell into being girlfriend and boyfriend without any premeditation, really. I remember the first time he kissed me after a school dance. I felt him hard down below against me and it scared me to death. I actually almost passed out, and he pushed himself against me and kissed me harder."

Each and every one of us has our own X-rated movies from our past that we can replay over and over again in the privacy of our own minds, of our own step-by-step progression into the lustful, passionate, steamy, erotic realms of sexual intimacy. Life itself is the ultimate X-rated experience. But instead of feeling there is anything wrong with our own totally graphic sex scenes that we have acted out in our past with various lovers, it is important to look back with positive feelings, with reverence, with a good sense of humor of course—and also with complete acceptance of how we felt and behaved during each stage of our sexual and spiritual unfolding.

What was your tale of early sexual passion and sometimes excruciating embarrassment? How did you push and stumble your way into the first touches, the first kisses of your pubescent years? I encourage you once again to pause and look honestly back to your first real love affair, where you held tentative hands, experienced visual intercourse of passionate intensity, kissed and pressed breasts against chest. Open yourself to feel the emotional rushes that came to you back then . . . let yourself remember the pure bliss of knowing someone loved you totally and you loved them totally as well . . . and yes, after fully reliving the entire span of your first pristine romance, also relive the breaking up of the romance, so that you can free yourself of any lingering contractions that your first major heartbreak might have caused inside you.

Going All the Way

Virginity used to be a commodity that could carry a very high price tag in traditional societies where a girl was required to be sexually untouched if she was to find a suitable husband. Even just a few decades ago in our own culture, the prevailing ethos was that a girl should be a virgin when she entered into wedlock. From an idealistic, mystic point of view, this vision of the perfect eternal marriage of two pure souls holds a great deal of appeal with youngsters, and as a mythic dream it carries remarkable potency.

Reality however almost never plays itself out on pristine mythic turf. I would guess that less than 1 percent of all married couples in our country right now are first-time lovers. High school sweethearts don't tend to stay together, especially where so many students leave for college. We tend to have three, five, ten lovers or more before settling into married life. And a large minority of people run through several marriage partners before finding one with whom they can live happily for the long-term haul.

I remember reading a novel back when I was in college in the mid-sixties, a sometimes magical book by a gifted young man named Richard Fariña, who in his short life recorded two very fine folk albums, wrote one compelling book (later made into a film), and then at the age of twenty-nine rode his motorcycle over a cliff and was gone forever. Somewhere in the middle of his book, *Been Down So Long It Looks Like Up to Me*, he introduced the notion that although his main character has had dozens of sexual encounters and plunged repeatedly to the depths of the female mystery on physical levels, he still considers himself a spiritual virgin, since he has not yet surrendered his heart to any of his girlfriends. He is searching for a girl who is likewise virginal, but, in typical chauvinistic logic, he requires that she be a physical virgin as well as a spiritual one.

This book sold hundreds of thousands of copies in college towns, capturing the imaginations and mythic visions of a great many of us. Right in the middle of the sexual revolution, we were still dreaming of virginal relationships and feelings. There is certainly something sacrosanct about the ultimate act of sexual communion.

Perhaps most of us at one time or another dreamed of

being fulfilled through the traditional myth of virginal wedlock. But regardless of our deeper visions of mystic purity,
at some point most of us lost our virginity long before we
found a compatible mate.

Do you remember that first young man or young
woman who took your virginity from you? As you look
back, notice whether you felt somehow violated when you
made love for the first time, or whether you surrendered
freely, or perhaps even projected your desires onto your
sexual partner. How deeply can you recall your own first
full bouts of sexual intercourse? Who was that person you
first bared yourself to and merged your body with? Take
time to relive all the various emotional passions that overwhelmed you before, during, and after the intercourse experience. Remember vividly how you felt at the moment you
lost your virginity . . . and remember specifically how you
felt afterward.

Lovers Come and Lovers Go

After the first, how many other lovers have there been in
your life with whom you've shared your most precious sexual intimacies? I've known people who have made love with
no one but their wife or husband their entire lives. I've
known others who claim to have had myriad lovers by the
age of twenty-four. You, like me, are probably somewhere
in between these extremes.

It is a well-documented psychological observation that a
person's first few intimate relationships tend to be primarily
mutual-therapy involvements when viewed from a profes-

sional perspective. As we leave our homes and venture out into the world as young adults, we are almost always packing a variety of inhibitions and hang-ups inherited from our familial background. This is just how life is.

A major dimension of our early adulthood years is in fact our struggle to resolve the contractions, the hostilities, the feelings of resentment, of loss, of heartbreak and abuse that we carry in our hearts from childhood. We are all more or less neurotic as young adults, in that we are functioning half from honest direct responses to the present moment and half from distorted unconscious reactions programmed into us as children. Growing up and reaching maturity means resolving these lingering childhood traumas, letting go of bitter feelings, discharging buried emotions, and moving on into our own independent adult life.

Each new romantic relationship, if viewed clearly, is a definite learning process. Even the relationships that end as disasters have their crucial lessons to teach us. If we learn the lesson at hand, we move forward. If we don't learn the lesson, we tend to repeat the same patterns in our next relationship. An old Sufi saying from the dervish tradition of Turkey says that "each new moment is our teacher with its wisdom to offer us. And each of us will find ourselves hit over the head by the same staff repeatedly until we learn the lesson at hand."

In this light, I encourage you to look back over your past love affairs with a new perspective in the weeks and months to come. Reflect on what you actually learned from each person with whom you shared sexual intimacies. Instead of fixating only upon the stimulating sexual memories, or upon the pain of separation when the learning experience had run its course, learn to focus your power of attention clearly upon the deep heart lessons you were taught by former lovers. In this way you can purify your heart from old wounds, and amplify the beauty and blessing of each past sexual encounter.

The Healing Heart Meditation

I want to teach you at this point a truly magical emotional-healing program that you can readily apply to your own life as a regular practice if you so choose. The first step is to set aside between five minutes and half an hour on a regular basis, preferably every day in the beginning. Each day, choose one of the "memory excursion" themes I have offered in this chapter, or a similar one that comes to mind. Devote your total attention during each particular memory session to reliving and reflecting upon a particular intimate relationship you have experienced in your past. Spend half of each session reliving the experience vividly, and the other half reflecting upon the lessons learned from the relationship. You will find that these reflective memory excursions begin almost immediately to trigger deep healing in your current emotional and behavioral patterns.

The unavoidable truth is that the lingering contractions you feel in your heart over past relationships serve directly to inhibit your ability to expand and love at deeper levels in the present moment. To heal these old heartbreaks is therefore essential. Likewise, the love you recall and relive in your heart toward old lovers will immediately amplify the positive intensity of your current love relationship.

From a therapeutic point of view, this is especially true of your relationship with your own mother or father. For instance, if you are a woman and you carry hatred and resentment in your heart against your father, this negative energy will inevitably pollute your relationship with the present man in your life. Likewise if you are a man and feel hostility or rejection for your mother, you will be quite unable to truly relax and open up to the present woman in your life. This is a simple law of psychology, as well as a basic spiritual truth. Jesus made the point quite clearly when He suggested that we must go make peace with whomever in our family we feel hostility toward before we attempt anything of a spiritual nature out in the world.

What is essential, as Eva Pierrakos so succinctly pointed out in *The Pathwork of Self-Transformation*, is that we learn to look back to see clearly what it was that we didn't get from a past relationship. Otherwise we tend to continue trying to satisfy childhood needs in adult relationships. And the stark reality is that we simply cannot ever fulfill childhood needs once we have outgrown childhood. Instead, we must simply acknowledge and accept the less-than-perfect humanity of our parents and other childhood intimates. If possible we should also fully forgive everyone in our past, and let them off the guilt hook for not being what we needed at the time. Especially regarding parental contractions, Pierrakos has said, "survey all your past actions and reactions with new understanding and insight, whereupon you will release your parents. You will no longer need to be loved as you needed to be loved when you were a child. And since you are no longer a child now, you will seek love in a different way, by giving it instead of expecting it."

This is the deep switch that comes to us once we have moved through enough intimate relationships to clear ourselves of our childhood hang-ups. We stop acting like children, who by nature demand love, and begin to be self-sufficient adults who can give love unconditionally.

Right at this point in a person's life is where sexual intercourse suddenly becomes genuinely spiritual. When a relationship isn't just another acting out of our need for childish love, we finally move into position to relax, to reverse the flow of energy in our systems from take take take to give give take take give give give!

What Jesus and Mohammed and Buddha and all other great teachers of the heart path have been saying for thousands of years is that as soon as we start giving love without expecting any in return, we become purified channels for receiving and broadcasting into the world around us the universal love that fills the universe. What happens as we approach orgasm in a sexual encounter is that this universal love suddenly becomes a million times amplified for a brief time, purifying our souls more and more with each deep sexual encounter.

At this beautiful point, instead of a sexual involvement being therapeutic, it becomes transcendent. Finally we are no longer struggling to overcome old problems in our emotional lives. Instead, we are free to explore an entirely different dimension of life and love—a spiritual dimension that knows no bounds, that includes infinite ecstasy, that sheds insight on all our earthly situations, transporting us into heart spaces where the Spirit genuinely dwells within and is expressed through our own personal lives.

Curiously, couples who tap into this transcendent quality of lovemaking often speak of how, each time they make love with each other, it is as if for the first time. The feeling of being a virgin becomes a mystic quality at this level. As we come together and let go of thoughts and expectations, memories and projections, we lose our chronic sense of linear time and emerge into what scientists of quantum mechanics and the new physics call nonlinear time, where in fact the present moment is eternal, always new.

In this transformed level of consciousness, each new sex-

ual encounter carries us through the entire gamut of romantic and spiritual feelings of a lifetime; we experience
ourselves as bashful adolescent lovers with our first touch
and kiss of the encounter, and then progress through the
entire range of feelings and intimate interactions that lead
up to total full-blast orgasm.

"All I really need from life these days," a friend who is
very deeply in love with his wife told me recently, "is that
when I'm making love, it's always like for the first time.
That's how it is with Tanya and that's why things are so
good between us. Our sexual relationship really is what
holds everything together, in our money situation and everything else. What we've found is that especially if we sleep
apart most of the time, and don't just burn out on each
other through too much closeness, we keep the charge of
attraction high. And then when we do come together, it's
always new. We've somehow found something together, it's
hard to talk about. But with her, I can really just be who I
am, and I'm a person who always feels a little shy every time
it comes time to make love again, even if I've done it with
the same woman a hundred times already, which is about
how many times Tanya and I have. We were counting last
week just for fun, talking about how we both feel the same,
that if we take time each time, and let ourselves drop down
into a real quiet-feeling sort of place together in bed, then
I feel like I've never been inside her before—right when I'm
going into her, it's as if it's the first time, it's some sort of
absolutely pure experience. It's like you were just telling me,
about the spiritual side of lovemaking. It's definitely there,
and I don't know what I'd do if I didn't have Tanya to share
it with. It's such an amazing thing to feel like young lovers
at first, and then in the course of an evening plunge ourselves
totally into each other."

Let me give you space and time away from reading right

now if you wish, so you can look back in a relaxed manner and reflect on whichever of your past love affairs pops into mind related to the sharing of this "first time" feeling in sexual intimacy. Be aware of your breathing . . . your heartbeat . . . your emotions . . . and take off on a "memory expedition" to relive the depths of spiritual passion you have experienced while making love.

2

The Unbridled
Sexual Rush

Angela found herself fooling around in junior high school, drinking some beer or wine with her friends and sometimes getting loose enough to let one of the boys kiss her and feel her. She was by nature very shy sexually, but alcohol seemed to break her free of her usual inhibitions. Then in high school, she fell in love with a wild boy two grades ahead of her. This fellow was a baseball player and liked to drink scotch like his daddy did. Angela lost her virginity without hardly feeling anything, she was so looped. In college, everything seemed to change; she switched to smoking grass because it was a much more intense sexual rush right through her whole body. And when she graduated and started work, she got caught up with a group of friends using cocaine a few nights a week to boost their social and sexual thrills.

It's so dangerously easy these days to slip into the drug routines that dominate our culture. Many people consider the casual use of drugs, both legal and illegal, to be worthwhile. Drugs such as alcohol, marijuana, and cocaine do sometimes seem to push us beyond our inhibitions, stimulate our sexual feelings, and make it easier to surrender to our wild passions. So why not indulge in a drink or a puff or a line before getting down to sexual intimacies?

The simple psychological truth is that chronic use of drugs of any kind seriously tends to reduce rather than enhance our capacity for spiritual communion during lovemaking. Drugs can sometimes provide us with a wild breathless experience of sexual abandon, as we find ourselves doing things we usually are too inhibited to risk. By definition, drugs serve to numb our intimate sensibilities, however. That's why they reduce our inhibitions—they make us less aware of what we are doing, and turn off parts of our minds so that we can plunge blindly into oblivious sexual encounter.

It is my observation, as well as that of my colleagues, that when the use of drugs becomes a regular pattern in lovemaking, spiritual communion is almost always dulled out of existence. When couples habitually get high on one thing or another in order to provoke passionate feelings with each other, the relationship progressively withers and dies at deeper levels of heart contact.

Angela came to see me without letting her boyfriend know she was seeking advice about her drug problem. I was already working with a girlfriend of hers who was likewise trying to get beyond old drug habits and into a new, more rewarding sex life. Angela talked about this subject with her friend, and at the age of twenty-seven finally realized that life was passing her by in a cloud of druggy haze. She admitted to herself that sometime soon she wanted to settle down in life, establish the kind of sexual relationship she always was dreaming about but never quite attaining, and perhaps even have children.

"But I've tried over and over again to stop using drugs, and every time, I get pulled back into it," she told me at our first meeting in my office. "I'm not an addict, when I'm alone, I don't use anything at all usually. It's just when I go out with someone, and especially when it comes to sex. I'm afraid, that's all. And drugs get me beyond that feeling of trembling, of wanting to run away."

I asked her whether she had ever had a boyfriend who didn't use drugs, and she thought a moment, staring into space, remembering. "Twice," she said.

"And what happened with them?"

"It just never quite came alive. I would want a couple of glasses of wine with dinner, and then would get a little buzzed, and I guess they didn't like a girl who did that. It just doesn't work to have one person drinking and the other a teetotaler, does it?"

In most cases this is true. People who have gotten a bit looped on one thing or another are usually slightly foggy and insensitive, not completely present, and this is bothersome to someone who has taken nothing drugwise and is hungry for a deep intimate encounter. Of course, this same situation can also be viewed from the point of view of the person high on something, who will feel that the teetotaler is too inhibited, not loose enough, and perhaps overly judgmental.

The reality we all have had to face is that venturing into sexual intimacy with someone almost always does generate certain inhibitions and anxieties. Even in a successful long-term relationship, it is normal and even to be encouraged to feel a certain bashfulness when approaching one's lover anew. Human beings are by nature and also by cultural conditioning bashful about their sexual feelings and involvements. And we become especially shy creatures when we let ourselves open up to the ultimate vulnerability of spiritual nakedness when making love.

Krishnamurti often spoke of how we should nurture our sense of bashfulness as our most prized emotional quality. "People who cannot feel bashful cannot feel the true depths of life," he once said.

In the same way that we would bow our heads when in the presence of the supreme Godhead, we should naturally tend to feel reverence and awe in the presence of our own infinite sexual powers, and in the presence of our lover's sexuality as well. There is nothing more holy than joining our bodies together in sexual union with our lover. So shyness seems the proper emotion when initiating a new sexual encounter.

The problem for most of us is that along with our positive spiritual sense of shyness when approaching a bout of lovemaking, most of us also possess an inherited load of quite painful conditioned anxieties related to the sex act. If our parents were afraid of their own sexuality, for instance, then we picked this fear up very early in life, perhaps right at the moment of conception. Some psychologists have even suggested that if a child is conceived by a sexually anxious couple, this child will carry a feeling of contraction related to sexual intimacy right from the beginning.

Regardless of the influences of such feelings, once a child is born, family, community, and church attitudes tend to amplify a child's natural bashfulness into full-blown sexual anxieties.

"My mom was someone who couldn't hide her sexual feelings when my dad was around, she was a very passionate woman when I look back and remember her," Angela told me in a later session. "But she was also religious, and my dad was really religious to a fault. So Mom felt guilty when she felt sexy, and Dad felt the same way. I never even knew they did anything like making out or having intercourse until I was about ten and came downstairs one night and innocently stumbled upon them naked, with Dad on top of Mom. Mommy screamed when she saw me standing there watching, and I ran back upstairs. Nothing was ever said about the incident, but it left me even more afraid of sex than ever. When I came of age and got interested in boys, it took me a long time and quite a few beers before I'd even let a boy touch me. I'm like my mom, I have a lot of passion in me, I need to make love. It's just almost impossible for me to relax and let myself hang loose unless I drink or take something to push me beyond my inhibitions."

Like Angela, each of us was strongly influenced in our sexual attitudes and habits by our parents. Let me give you a few moments right now to look back and remember your parents as lovers. Were they open and healthy in letting you see their feelings of sexual attraction toward each other, or were they afraid and ashamed of their sexuality, hiding it from you?

Pause . . . relax . . . see what memories spring to life as you take off on a deep, reflective memory expedition focused on this theme.

Sex Without Restraint

It's important to keep in mind that our sexual identity is not a quality with which we are born. Up until puberty, we are very busy developing a sense of who we are that is quite devoid of an overt sexual dimension. Our adolescent personality becomes formed, our ego structured, our vision of ourselves solidified in our young mind—and then out of nowhere, around the age of twelve, we are suddenly assaulted by overwhelming sexual feelings and passionate physiological transformations that seem quite alien to our already-established sense of who we are.

Puberty is without doubt the most overpowering rite of passage in a human being's life. And yet, as prominent psychologists such as Robert Klein point out, our culture is almost entirely lacking any structured community ritual that would help youngsters to weather their internal pubescent hurricanes successfully.

In contrast, most primitive societies, as anthropologists have discovered, openly and actively focused community attention upon the coming-of-age experience. Through participating in powerful pubescent spiritual rituals, youngsters were able to gain the support and social acknowledgment needed to develop a solid new sense of identity as sexually mature adults in the community.

Nowadays, children come of age in a vague, surreptitious manner. It is considered of no societal importance when a girl starts menstruating, for instance, or a boy starts ejaculating. There is no longer any inkling of spiritual significance to these primal new developments in a youngster's life. A budding adult's newborn fertility and ability to create the next generation receive almost no community acknowledgment or guidance.

Thus abandoned, the teenager of our society usually tries to downplay his or her internal sexual explosions and confusions. And lacking church or familial guidance of an honest up-front nature, the youngster is forced to turn to media inputs, to television and contemporary music for guidance, even though this realm of cultural instruction is often seriously lacking in any spiritual feel for the true nature of sexual awakening.

Teenagers also quite naturally turn to one another, especially to kids a few years older, for some semblance of understanding of how their sexual energies should be integrated into their sense of self. It is amazing how sex stories pass around at school, how lessons are learned or mislearned through rumors, dirty jokes, pornographic pictures, and in-group gossip. It's remarkable that anyone in our present society manages to get through the teen years with any mythic, romantic sexual feelings still intact.

Still, in spite of all the media distortions and societal disinterest in the rites of sexual passage, there does continue to exist a powerful ingrained mythic purity to the youthful spirit. Certain primal hungerings of the human heart and soul seem to be our genetic inheritance. Each new generation, regardless of the presence or lack of a formal rite of sexual passage, discovers as if for the first time the enduring mystery of a potent spiritual identity to be found right in the very center of budding sexual passions. No matter how demeaning the media might try to make sex, no matter how boring and mundane sex-ed classes might portray the sex act, no matter how druggy things might get or how religiously inhibited, still each pubescent youngster feels deep inside a bright, explosive, infinite sense of promise in his or her sexual unfolding. Sex looms ahead as the eternal gateway to paradise, the romantic vehicle that will transform mundane reality into the mystic world that all youngsters sense must exist beyond the drabness of regular life.

You went through your own unique transformation when sexuality overwhelmed you in your early teen years. You experienced all the sudden flushes of wonder and also embarrassment at your own biological awakenings. You found yourself seemingly possessed by a power that sometimes threatened to drive you literally crazy.

If you were a boy, you almost certainly found yourself plagued with such pubescent fears as that of getting an erection that would be noticed by people around you; for instance, in class if you felt yourself suddenly getting turned on by the sight of a girl's body in the seat in front of you. The sad fact is that instead of being allowed to feel proud of your masculinity, proud of your potency, you were conditioned instead to be afraid to let anyone see that you had become a man. You felt there was something definitely against the rules, something dirty, something pornographic, something religiously sinful about your totally natural tendency to get an erection. And this negative conditioning related to your sexual potency made you feel all sorts of inhibitions—which you at some point quite probably discovered you could temporarily obliterate with a few beers or perhaps a couple of puffs or a few lines.

If you were a girl, the situation was sometimes even more excruciatingly embarrassing. I have known girls trying to pretend that coming into sexual womanhood is no big thing, that there's no anxiety involved. It's hip to play cool. And of course these days, there are some youngsters who do have parents who are sexually open and positive, and so some children do go through puberty without becoming overly uptight about their budding sexuality.

Most girls, however, even if their parents are open about sexual things, become bashful about their own nakedness when puberty comes. And this sudden bashfulness, this unexpected realization of their immense sexual presence, is the source of all later romantic and intimate feelings.

Take a break and see what memories come flooding into your mind as you look back to your own bashfulness in your teen years. Remember the actual rush of the natural high generated by the biochemical surgings of your sex hormones.

The Hunters and the Hunted

Once your sexual energies came into dominance after puberty, you advanced from being a child to being a new participant in the eternal hunt for a sexual partner that defines all of human civilization. The very nature of sexual mating is rooted in the spirit of the hunt. Traditionally, the hunt was seen as extremely one-sided, with supposedly weak feminine damsels being hunted down by potent masculine warriors. In actual practice these days, though, both sides of the bargain are the hunters, and both are at the same time being hunted.

"It was such a scary feeling just to walk down the corridors at school," Angela told me one afternoon. "I could feel eyes on me even from the back, and then I would look around and some boy would be walking behind me, eyeing me. Everyone was hunting for someone special to fulfill their romantic dreams. That's what high school was all about. That's what almost all of life is all about."

Angela learned around the age of fifteen that she could deal successfully with the situation at school. She even discovered that because she was quite beautiful, she could push her way around, hunt down particular boys and make them feel bashful by getting them all flustered and hot for her. That was fun.

As things progressed after school and on weekends, however, the flirting got more serious, and the boys got more passionate and pushy. "At first, I would just be cold and turn them off as quick as I could," she confessed. "But that wasn't really what I wanted at all. Then I found out that beer could transform the situation. I could drink just one bottle and then suddenly everything would become different. Reality would shift in directions that left me feeling absolutely magnificent. I still remember those early parties, they were crazy, we had a great time. I would go to them uptight as could be, but somebody always had some beers, and the boys knew I was fun if we drank a little. That's how all this got started. And I've just never managed to stop it. I'm still afraid of making love unless I've got some sort of buzz on. I'm afraid I wouldn't feel turned on at all."

Our natural sexual responses, when unimpeded by inhibitions, are of course largely a matter of genetic programmings that push us toward sexual intercourse. The survival of our species depends on men and women copulating often enough to produce a new generation. In every animal species, there is a certain ingrained hunting process that either provokes the male to chase the female or the other way around. Human beings are simply acting out the essential reproduction boogie with all their great sexual forays. And culturally ingrained fears and sexual anxieties only muddy the instinctive responses of lovemaking.

So the primitive hunt for a sexual partner continues even in the midst of our supposedly civilized society. And unfortunately, relationships usually emerge in the midst of fairly low-level seduction games that have come to define our mating ritual in contemporary society. As we will see in later chapters, it is essential in a relationship to learn to transcend the shallow games of encounter and seduction that too often define the beginning of a sexual partnership. Otherwise intimate relating simply is not possible. And because drugs are so often caught up in the initial hunting scene, they must be put aside as well in order to plunge beyond the facade of the hunt.

What have you usually been in sexual relating—the hunter or the hunted? Have you preferred to be the one selecting your choice and going actively into hunting gear to get whom you want sexually, or have you played mostly the hunted, the luring morsel that stimulates the sexual-hunting instincts in those around you?

And in your relationship now, are you still locked into these early-romance habits of playing hunter-hunted roles while making love, or do you quickly advance beyond your initial role-playing games and into deeper realms of encounter?

Birth Control

The stark reality of life on this planet right now, which directly provokes the use of birth-control methods in general, is that there are already far too many people being born. We are therefore not under pressure to crank out a baby every two years in order to feel we are doing our job in keeping our species afloat. Just the opposite has become the vision of a great many couples—that we do best if we have just one or two or three children, and give them all the love and attention we can so that they can lead full, happy, and also perhaps powerful and influential lives from an ecological point of view.

Therefore the question of birth control naturally arises as a key theme in a heterosexual love relationship. There are several alternatives, with varying degrees of effectiveness and side effects. The completely natural path to birth control, where a woman keeps track of her temperature and mucous condition to determine when ovulation occurs, and abstains from sexual relating when she is fertile, is perhaps ideal but at the same time very difficult to manage during times of emotional upset and stress. On the other hand, the IUD has proven itself somewhat dangerous for many women and downright deadly for others. New miracle pills to make men infertile are still of questionable health value, likewise the "morning after" pill for women. Tying the tubes is of course another possibility, but it is of limited application for couples who want to leave the option open for having children in the future.

This leaves us with the pill, the condom, and the diaphragm. The limited question I wish to address here is this: How do each of these three influence spiritual intimacy in sexual relating?

In terms of getting in the way of actual intimate relating during intercourse, the pill and the diaphragm are of course much better to use than the condom, since putting the condom on the penis requires a break in the flow and intensity of lovemaking. The condom is also an obvious physical barrier between male and female, an artificial addition to mother nature that takes away the direct contact of the most sensitive sexual parts of human anatomy. This is not to say that condoms block spiritual intercourse, but they do make it a bit harder on some levels. Of course, when there is any danger of a sexually transmitted disease, it is important to use condom protection.

The pill seems at first glance ideal. The woman just pops a tiny pill in the morning and that's that—no mess, no worry—the perfect medical solution. However, when we look closely to see how a woman's biochemical and emotional presence is altered by the pill, it becomes obvious that there are serious drug drawbacks to this form of birth control, from several layers of concern.

I won't bother to review the medical dangers of birth-control pills, since I assume you know them from the popular media coverage. The level of concern we are exploring here is the way in which a woman loses touch with her natural feminine identity, her relationship with her cyclic procreative energies. When taking birth-control pills, a woman is in essence always in the pregnant mode both physiologically and emotionally. The monthly egg doesn't drop. There is no feeling of being fertile once a month, of being vibrant with the potential to become pregnant.

"What I remember is that back when I was on the pill, I was always in limbo," a former client of mine told me recently. "I started taking the pill when I was sixteen; my mother thought she was doing me a favor, being so liberal-minded. And I took them for eleven years before I realized what I was doing to myself. Then when I stopped, what a world of difference it made in my life. I felt I came alive, slowly to be sure, but after about six months, I felt I was a woman for the first time, as if the pill had kept me from really discovering what sex was all about. Now I feel my potency, my power to get pregnant if I want to—I'm a real woman! And I go through so many deep emotional changes each month. What a rush it is to feel myself ready to drop an egg, and then to feel that day when I'm definitely fertile. It makes lovemaking always new, never the same."

I know that many of you reading this book are probably taking birth-control pills. I hesitate to say what I am saying, because the choice of using birth-control pills is an extremely personal one. Many women overcome the emotional drawbacks of the pill, transcend the physiological effects of the drug, and enter into very deep spiritual communion with their lover/mate while on the pill.

At the same time, I do feel the responsibility in a book such as this to speak the truth as I see it, as I have especially seen it through the eyes of lovers and female clients struggling with this issue of birth control over the years. At a certain point, most women who are seeking new intimate depths to their sexual lives at least experiment with putting aside the pill and using alternate forms of birth control to see whether there is a noticeable difference.

Sex with a Diaphragm

Specifically related to spiritual awakening during intercourse, my observation has been that most women end up preferring the diaphragm over other methods of birth control, once they learn to use it in ways that ensure a high level of genuine contraceptive protection. The diaphragm has the obvious benefit over the pill of not influencing a woman's emotional and physiological condition. And in contrast to the condom, it can be put in place hours before a sexual encounter, and never thought about during intercourse.

Especially when used in conjunction with natural birth-control methods, the diaphragm proves itself really quite adequate in preventing pregnancy. Most women I know seem to prefer to use it all the time, except during menstruation. One of the certain ways to ruin a sexual encounter is for the woman and/or the man to be worrying about whether an unwanted pregnancy will result from intercourse.

A woman is, of course, wise to get to know herself at the

level recommended by the natural birth-control methods; then she can detect at least most of the time when she is ovulating, and abstain from intercourse for that one particular day when she is most likely to become pregnant. This particular day is experienced by most women as a very high time spiritually as well as sexually—but to risk intercourse, even with the diaphragm in place, is to add a certain element of worry to the sexual experience. What I have found is that abstaining during this day once a month becomes a sexual fast of importance for a woman and a man—an acknowledgment of the procreative powers they are encountering when making love.

The third element to successful birth control with a diaphragm is this—a clear, honest assessment on the part of the man as well as the woman regarding their true feelings concerning pregnancy. A woman who unconsciously hungers for a baby but who consciously denies to herself this desire will often find ways to undermine her birth-control program. Again, the clear seeing of oneself, as Joel Kramer advises, is the key to contraceptive success as well as to spiritual expansion. The diaphragm works as an excellent, trustworthy aid as long as there is the clear intent to make love without making babies.

Kundalini Semen Control

In the ancient religious traditions of Yogic and Tantric meditation in India and Tibet, and likewise in the heritage of Taoism in China, there exists a powerful sexual practice for men in which the semen is completely controlled and never allowed to emerge from the tip of the penis. As one of the modern masters of this technique, Mantak Chia, has explained in his book *Taoist Secrets of Love*, "the average American male ejaculates 5,000 times in his lifetime, equal roughly to 4 gallons of fluid. This amount of sperm is enough to pollinate one trillion female eggs."

The energy used to create a single sperm cell is considerable. Mantak Chia estimates that each sexually active male uses nearly one-third of his overall vital energy in order to produce continually the 300 million spermatozoa that are released with each ejaculation. From a spiritual point of view, therefore, it is highly advisable that a man learn to come less often, to hold his charge, and to rechannel in directions that directly stimulate spiritual awakening the energies saved by not ejaculating.

I am not going to advise that all American men learn to withhold their sperm when making love, since the seminal-withholding feat is an arduous though highly rewarding spiritual undertaking. Therefore, we cannot realistically look to this technique as the next new breakthrough in birth-control methods.

However, as we will be seeing step by step in this discussion, a man has a great deal of responsibility when making love, in learning to break free of his compulsive masturbatory patterns of pushing for quick physical release. In the opposite direction, spiritual sexuality involves a shifting of attention and devotion away from the ejaculation experience, and into the preejaculation experience, where the sexual charging of the human nervous system can be used to activate more spiritual dimensions of heart-to-heart encounter.

Pause if you want to and look back to all the sexual encounters you have had, in light of this contraceptive theme we have just been discussing. What have your own experiences been? Do you agree with me, or have your experiences proven different results? I offer this section not to dictate behavior concerning contraceptives but to stimulate reflection.

Effects of Different Drugs
During Intercourse

Briefly, we should reflect here on the several different types of drugs commonly used in our culture, and consider how they directly affect sexual relating and spiritual unfolding. My observations and even the statistical studies I am referring to do not always hold true in individual cases, so please don't feel judged if my estimation of a particular chemical additive to the human system is different from yours.

Let's take cocaine first. Cocaine is certainly one of the most talked-about drugs in recent years. "I just love it when me girlfriend rubs some on the tip of me wong and then kisses me with lips that make me numb, and then we can go and go and go and I take me time in coming, that's what's pleasing to me. The stuff makes me a champion," one fellow told me. "And when I'm going to a party and I'm feeling a bit nervous you know, just a quick snort and I'm on my feet and the talk of the town. Not that I do it all the time mind you, I know it's dangerous and all that. But it is an excellent pick-me-up, don't you agree?"

I held my peace and didn't argue with him, although my vision of cocaine, reinforced through working over the years with perhaps hundreds of clients with cocaine problems, has been that coke is a let-me-down, not a pick-me-up drug. It directly numbs not only the penis and lips but also the heart.

People using coke tend to become progressively less able to enter into deep intimate relationships. The drug is one of the true tragedies of modern times in this regard.

The same is equally true of all the uppers and downers alike that proliferate both legally through the medical profession's drug-pushing habits and illegally through other channels. Quaaludes, for example, were considered fantastic sexual boosters in the seventies, but proved to be just the opposite when used more than a few times. Speed likewise can sometimes turn lovemaking into a wild, endless bout of almost coming. But the experience is almost always devoid of any redeeming spiritual overtones.

Many folks over the age of fifty are taking sleeping pills regularly, as are a smaller but significant portion of the under-fifty population. These medications, as I have already pointed out in *Secrets of a Good Night's Sleep*, absolutely demolish one's sexual appetites, and likewise numb and confuse the spiritual sensibilities of higher consciousness. Wherever possible, it is far better to seek nondrug vehicles for release from insomnia, so that the cutting edge of spiritual awareness remains intact.

In the late sixties and seventies, psychedelic drugs were lauded as the ultimate sexual/spiritual experience. Many people did have remarkable times, since chemicals such as LSD, mescaline, and peyote blast normal consciousness into radical new realms of perception. There is no doubt that such chemicals have vast power in "shifting the assemblage point" of consciousness into realms often considered spiritual.

However, again the reality is this: The energy expended in taking such drugs can use up spiritual reserves that would otherwise be used over entire years. I did research for the National Institutes of Mental Health, studying this phenomenon in the late sixties, working with certain subjects who seemed to be integrating occasional psychedelic usage successfully into their sexual relationships—and also working with many clients who were so burned out from psychedelic abuse that they were veritable basket cases when it came to sexual and spiritual relating.

At a lower level of intensity, tens of millions of people in the last couple of decades have been claiming that marijuana is the ultimate drug for sexual charging. Contrary to the *Playboy* reports that using grass made people impotent, religious traditions from the East have in fact praised the ways in which occasional use of cannabis can stimulate a flow of energy up and down the spine, awakening the different energy centers, or chakras, in the body, and making sexual intercourse quite amazingly powerful.

With marijuana as with other drugs, however, there exists a crucial energetic trade-off that often goes completely unmentioned. When certain dimensions of consciousness are heightened by a drug, other dimensions are equally suppressed. There is always this dynamic in drug-induced approaches to sexual/spiritual awakening, as opposed to nondrug approaches such as I am highlighting in this book.

With marijuana, a man's balls, for instance, often come afire soon after smoking. He becomes a powerhouse of a lover at times, able to go and go for hours before coming. However, the heart chakra, the emotional center of the nervous system, is usually impaired during such sexual rushes caused by marijuana. Always certain crucial dimensions of consciousness are lost in order to gain the rush desired.

I want to suggest now that you look back over just the last month of your life. Make mental note of how many times you have taken a drug, any drug at all. . . . How do you evaluate the effects of these drug intakes on your sexual/spiritual level of awareness and activity? . . . Venture into a deep memory expedition back to the last few times you have

made love, and see how often during the last month or so
you were under the influence of something, rather than clear
in mind and emotion, body and soul . . . and then after all
this reflection, let your mind ruminate deeply about how
you want to continue or modify your use of drugs in your
sexual relating in the days and weeks to come.

All Things in Moderation

The challenge drugwise offered in this book, if in fact you
find you have a bit of a drug hang-up attached to your sexual
relating, is to take several moderate steps in the direction of
using drugs less and less in your intimate encounters. If
indeed you have a serious drug problem, certainly the best
step is to seek professional help in your community. If your
problem is less intense, you can quite probably succeed on
your own in mastering the fine art of moderation in your
life. Once you begin to realize the great payoff of drugless
sex, you will have positive reinforcement for putting the
drugs aside in your love life.

However, it is always somewhat of a scary step to venture
more deeply into the emotional and spiritual nakedness that
comes when a drug habit related to sexual intercourse is
dropped. Many of you of course don't have this problem at
all. But for those of you who do, the anxiety associated with
facing your lover unaided by a couple of glasses of wine or
whatever has been your support vehicle can be quite great.

Throughout this book, for all the different dimensions of
sexual/spiritual relating we will be exploring, I will be saying
the same basic thing over and over again: You have plenty
of time; don't be in a great hurry to transform parts of your

life that you feel need alteration; set realistic goals one at a time, and advance through a number of attainable steps. And enjoy each step along the way, since there is no absolute end point you are going to reach, anyway.

In each of the seven dimensions we are exploring, the path to growth and realization through sexual relating involves putting away old habits, attitudes, memories, fantasies, and the like, so that you enter more fully into the intensity of your own biological and spiritual processes that sexual stimulation amplifies. In this chapter, we are quite simply aiming toward the putting aside of drugs that interfere with intimacy.

In the weeks to come, you as a responsible adult can take it upon yourself to look honestly at your habits in this regard, and progressively to reduce your dependence on drugs. What is liable to happen? Let's listen to Angela, with whom we started this chapter, as she talks about her first drugless sexual encounter.

"Richard actually asked me what was wrong when I told him last night that I'd rather have a Coke with dinner instead of our usual wine. I told him nothing was wrong, I just didn't feel like any alcohol. He went ahead and had a couple of glasses himself. I was amazed at how hard it was to keep from joining him. When we went home, I was nervous as could be at first, and he was a bit grumpy, feeling I was somehow rejecting him when I didn't join him for a smoke either. We've had our ritual of sleeping together every weekend for months now, and always we've done the same things. I was afraid of what might happen, so I just did what you advised me in our last session, and just took off my clothes and got into bed and relaxed, not thinking that anything at all sexually had to happen. Richard showered and I was half asleep when he came to bed. I'd been lying there watching my breathing and paying attention to just my body like you suggested, and I found myself feeling very good actually. And when he joined me, it all happened very surprisingly well, except that he was a bit of a brute—he always is—but this time I was a little bothered by him at first. Then I just relaxed and let him take me and it was, well, *exceptional* must be the right word for it. I was such a different person, my body hardly seemed like my own, my skin was so sensitive that everything he did to me felt delicious. But then he came too soon and that was that for him, he rolled off as usual and fell asleep almost instantly. Alcohol does that to him. I lay there a long time, thinking, remembering a whole bunch of things, men I had been with in the past, things like that. I felt proud of myself for having gone to bed with a man without a drink or a smoke. But I didn't feel close to Richard and that bothered me. Something has to give between us, I can see that. He uses drugs a lot, he's got a lot of energy, but he'll be old before his time. Me, I don't know, I have this feeling that something big is happening to me and I've just got to ride it out to the end regardless of the consequences. But I know that stopping or at least moderating my drinking and smoking is the first step."

A Beginning Overview

As you begin to reduce your own drug intake, if this is something you need to deal with, you will find that you are putting yourself on the experiential line as you face your old habits of relating and see yourself in a new light. You will also see your lover in a new light. The challenge is to accept this new vision that comes to you, and to let it influence both your feelings and your behavior in quite spontaneous ways.

I had been working with Angela for several sessions before she felt ready to make the step of reducing her drinking and smoking while making love. Likewise, you will probably want to read through this entire book to gain the full vision of how you can best venture into new ways of interacting with your lover before applying the suggestions of any one chapter to your own love life. Only when put altogether into a cohesive whole do the various suggestions come alive as an integral part of your intimate sharings with your lover.

Now that we have taken at least a preliminary view of the topics of healing old heartbreaks and moderating old drug habits, we are in position to move directly into the excitement of the unfolding present moments of your current love life. We will do this by looking at your ability to converse intimately with your sexual partner; to reveal yourself through visual intercourse; to quiet your talking and thinking mind as you get skin-to-skin; and to put all expectations and fantasies aside while you move into full sexual intercourse and spiritual communion.

Rather than my giving you a specific theme to reflect upon to end this chapter, it might prove more worthwhile to do the following "open reflection" meditation. After reading this paragraph, put the book aside . . . tune into your breathing and whole-body presence as you get comfortable . . . be aware of yourself as a body . . . as a sexual and spiritual being . . . and allow your mind to reflect spontaneously on anything we have talked about thus far.

3

More Intimate Conversations

Matt was the owner of his own company by the time he turned twenty-nine, and on the surface he appeared to be quite satisfied with his life. He was a great talker and salesman and also a hot ladies' man, seeming to be able to get about any woman on whom he set his sights. But deep down, he was a lonely man, able to manipulate people quite easily but unable to break out of his put-on personality and talk from the heart with anyone. As a result, he found himself drifting from one short sexual involvement to the next without ever dropping into the deeper intimacies that he craved.

All true heart relationships are built upon the foundation of honest vocal communications spoken in confidence between close friends. If we don't manage to establish a sense of trust and intimate interface when speaking to someone, there is little chance of attaining sexual satisfaction when clothes come off and words fall away. As Lorna and Phillip Sarrel, two Yale University researchers, concluded in a recent article in *The Redbook Report on Sexual Relationships*, "the ability to share thoughts and feelings about sex with your partner is the single factor most highly correlated with a good sexual relationship."

A great many of us however, in the process of growing up, developed isolating communication habits that hide our true feelings behind a slick but somehow phony verbal mask, especially when we find ourselves relating with someone who excites us with romantic possibilities. To one extent or another, almost all of us learned to play conversational games that make us appear more suave and sophisticated, more casual and in charge of things than we might feel under the surface of our vocal facade. And unfortunately, once an intimate affair gets locked into these shallow levels of conversational relating, it is often difficult to break through the joking and verbal game playing so as to achieve a deeper sharing of our feelings and thoughts with our lover.

Almost always, the progression toward full sexual intercourse involves considerable verbal intercourse. When this verbal intimacy is not adequately deep, very often the sexual encounter remains shallow. In a 1987 survey of women's sexual problems reported in *The Anatomy of Sex and Power*, Shere Hite found that "virtually all women listed their number-one problem to be lack of verbal communication with their partners."

Matt's last girlfriend, Clancy, happened to be a client of mine when she met and fell in love with him, so I got a weekly update on how she was faring in her new heart adventure. She told me she could see a deep and beautiful soul under Matt's great show of superficial glibness. Because she felt she could break through to his true self, she was willing to struggle with him rather than just dumping him as she had found herself ready to do several times.

Luckily, she met him right when he was ready to risk growing beyond his old habits of noncommunication. He'd been observing his own actions more and more over the last few years, and he knew that something was keeping him from dropping deeper into heartfelt relationships. At first he was defensive when Clancy tried to point to certain of his conversational habits that constantly interfered with a deepening of their intimate relationship. But her love for him was so bright that he was able to open up step by step and listen to her new insights regarding communications skills and emotional sharing.

"I don't think he's ever before really told anyone in his life what he was feeling deep down," she mentioned to me one morning during a session. "And I must say, I met his mom last Sunday and she's much worse than he is, chattering all the time, never revealing her real self at all. We had lunch with his whole family—twenty people I think were there for a big feast—and they were all jokers, seeing who could outjive the other. Matt and I had talked the night before about his family, and I could see during the luncheon that he was watching everyone with sharp eyes. His father didn't talk at all, by the way, he's the completely silent sort of man. And afterward when Matt and I went over to my place, Matt seemed temporarily frozen in his father's image, unable to open up at all. It took him about half an hour, but finally he got down to admitting how lonely he'd felt as a kid in his family. Then the most beautiful thing happened, look at me, I'm blushing just thinking about it. Right in the middle of his near-tears confession, we found ourselves suddenly so hungry for each other, we popped buttons getting at each other, it was the deepest I've felt with a man.

I'm afraid I'm ten times more in love with him than before. It's scary, but it's what I want."

The Magic Listener

You perhaps have heard already that many of the most powerful therapy techniques being used throughout the world are based on a therapist simply allowing a client to continue speaking for an entire session without the therapist interrupting to say anything at all except perhaps an occasional "Um-hmm, that's interesting, go on." In a vibrant relationship, the same dynamic is almost always present. When one person has something to say, the other doesn't interrupt the flow of words until the first person has had his or her say. This is how the true depths of heart contact are attained during intimate conversations.

What brought Matt to the point where he could finally speak at least a bit from the heart was that Clancy, right at that point in her life, was actively learning how to be a good listener. Instead of playing into his glib conversational antics, she would let him talk himself out, and then allow a silence to come between them—an experience that was quite new to Matt as well as to Clancy.

"In the middle of these sometimes uncomfortable silences," she told me, "would suddenly arise feelings and thoughts that were very special. I would see that he was plunging into unusual emotions, and then I would ask him if he would tell me what was going on inside him. When he managed to start talking, his entire voice was different, choked up sometimes, angry sometimes, but sincere, vulnerable, lovable."

The sad fact was that no one had really been available to listen to Matt when he was a little boy. This happens so often in modern families, especially for children who are number three or four or five, where the bigger kids are already getting most of the attention in the family. Television likewise is a great killer of family conversations, to a point where many psychologists are crying out against television as the number-one intimacy killer in our society. As long as the TV is on in a room, no one is really available to listen to a child when feelings bubble up, hungering for verbal expression.

This was the other side of Matt's problem: He was a terrible listener, afraid to be quiet long enough for someone he was with to drop down to deep conversational levels of intimacy. His parents had been afraid of such verbal sharing, so he was too, without even realizing it.

"At one point I had to tell him three times in a row that I was ready to drop him if he didn't shut up long enough so I could say what was on my mind," Clancy told me at one point. "Finally he started catching himself—it's all a matter of self-awareness, and thank God he's sharp enough to learn it."

The struggle that Matt and Clancy went through in order to attain intimacy at the conversational level is a struggle that most couples plough through successfully if they are to stay together and flourish in their relationship. You most surely have struggled in your own relationships in this regard. Before we go further into the dynamics of verbal intercourse, let me give you a breather to look back over your relationships and assess your own level of honesty and vulnerability when talking with your lover.

Speaking from the Heart

Leo Buscaglia has stated in *Loving Each Other* that "communication, the art of talking with each other, saying what we feel and mean, saying it clearly, listening to what the other says and making sure that we're hearing accurately, is by all indications the skill most essential for creating and maintaining loving relationships."

What is it, in fact, that transforms a simple conversation with someone into an intimate experience? How is it possible that some people can say so much and affect us so little, while others can say just a few words and touch us so deeply?

The human voice is a remarkable, multidimensional communications apparatus. It can broadcast from our inner realms of consciousness not only statistical data, plans of attack, and complex philosophical structures. It carries the added potential to convey from one human being to another all the pervading emotional undercurrents of our thoughts.

There is great value in looking deeply enough into the dynamics of this emotional dimension of communication so that you can begin to observe these dynamics in action in your very next conversations. As in all other aspects of this spiritual-sexuality program, your heightened awareness of your own habits will prove to be the key that stimulates desired transformations within your intimate relationship.

First of all, we should reflect upon the obvious but often-overlooked fact that our spoken voice is a product of our habitual breathing patterns. Sounds are generated when we exhale. When we inhale, we are momentarily quiet. Thus even when we are talking, there are always regular short lapses of silence while we refill our lungs with air.

The power other people hear in our voice depends to a large extent on the depth, steadiness, and power of our breathing. If we are tight in our breathing, our voices will be shallow and constricted. Likewise, if we are blocking emotions and thus chronically controlling our breathing, our voices will be tense and lacking in honest emotional qualities.

Our genetic physiological inheritance, and even more importantly our childhood conditionings regarding acceptable vocal expressions, determine to a great extent our adult vocal capacities. Matt for instance had parents who spoke in a flat, emotionally constricted tone of voice, so he did too. The fact that he later learned to fake a big booming chummy facade to his constricted vocal personality made his condition even harder to reverse, because he had lost touch with the sad, anxious, angry little boy buried under his suave adult vocal exterior.

A great many of us have fallen victim to this self-deception, because we fool even ourselves with the habitual put-on qualities to our voices. We have in essence rejected the weakness and anxiety, the complaining and hopelessness, the anger and frustration that our childhood voices naturally hungered to express. We identify with our shallow adult acting roles, rather than facing the painful reality that we were perhaps less than happy as children.

Parents are often the specific cause of this phony vocal development in children. "We were supposed to be one big happy family," Matt told me when he began coming to sessions with Clancy. "Whenever any of us kids expressed feelings that were anything but positive, we were punished. So we all had to learn to put on phony faces."

The disastrous result of forcing kids to inhibit their spontaneous vocalizations is a chronic loss of contact with their intimate heart feelings. The voice is supposed to be our instant vehicle for blowing off emotional steam. When this natural venting of the entire range of emotions is inhibited, children actually lose touch with their own emotional selves, with their heart reality.

As a child, I remember spending several years on a cattle ranch right next to the Pima and Papago Indian reservations in southern Arizona. There, I first learned the Indian perception of most white people as humans without hearts. Throughout the Native American population from time immemorial, there has been an underlying assumption that the thinking process is not just a function of the analytical mind but also a function of the heart and the emotions associated with the heart. From the Indian point of view, when a person doesn't speak from the heart, this person is either crazy or a downright liar.

The general observation of the indigenous American population was that most of the white marauders who were invading the country almost never spoke from the heart but, instead, from the head. These invaders were thus out of touch with their intimate feelings. Such lack of emotional self-awareness on the part of the immigrants was, of course, extremely helpful when trying to overlook the fact that the Indians were being killed and displaced during the European conquest of America.

Much of the contemporary business world that most of us have to try to function within carries on this heartless institution, where the compulsive push of capitalism and its inherent sense of dog-eat-dog mentality forces us to harden our hearts in order to win at the competitive game. Most of us were brought up to fear that if we become too sensitive, too vulnerable with our feelings, too expansive in our heart's capacity for compassion, we might not be able to survive in the modern capitalistic world.

On the other hand, as I have mentioned already, to win the world businesswise and to lose the ability to have deep heart contact in the process is not actually a success story. I think deep down we all agree with the Indians. People who do not speak from the heart are in certain ways really crazy, out of touch with the true nature of human life on this beautiful planet.

This means that most of us are at least a bit crazy, in that we have been brought up to block our true feelings from attaining vocal expression. Now as we struggle to come into deeper sexual and spiritual intimacy with our mate or lover, we must deal with what has happened to us in terms of inhibited vocal communication, and do what we can to break through the impasse and emerge into a revitalized realm of verbal communion.

Pause and take another look at your own ability to speak from the heart, to reveal your true emotions, to share your deeper thoughts and feelings with your lover. Is your vocal personality presently quite rigid and afraid of exposing your true feelings?

Look back to the most recent conversation you had with your mate or lover. To what extent were you in touch with your own heart feelings? To what extent were you able to let the words of your mouth spread the feelings in your heart to your sexual partner?

Transcending Fears of Vocal Nakedness

How do we pragmatically learn to reverse old inhibitions so that our true feelings for someone we love can come bubbling out in words?

The process of learning to speak from the heart very often requires overcoming certain ingrained fears that hold us back from intimate verbal sharing. There is almost always a certain feeling of risk involved in opening up to deeper verbal sharing. This risk very often generates feelings of anxiety related to what might happen if we reveal a dimension of ourselves that we have been conditioned to fear and hide from others.

Franklin D. Roosevelt told his compatriots in his first inagural address, "The only thing we have to fear is fear itself." This is an ultimately important statement when seen from a psychological point of view. Chronic anxiety and insecurity are the great killers of emotional honesty. The fear reflex makes us contract, makes us freeze, makes us become temporarily unconscious. And once we make this fear reaction a chronic mental, emotional, and physical habit, we are quite obviously in no position for intimate relating. In fact, anxiety is the primary inhibiting agent in all spiritual relating.

Throughout this book, I am regularly suggesting that you turn your power of attention in directions that quite probably you were conditioned in childhood to avoid, for fear of seeing something that would be upsetting or threatening to your existing attitudes and behavior patterns. I am playing another of the key therapeutic roles here, that of encouraging you to risk entering into certain anxiety-provoking situations so that your danger can be faced and seen for what it is—and so personal growth can take place.

Our first reaction to such provocation is usually negative. Who wants to be pushed into encountering buried feelings and memories that might be painful to see head-on? And who wants to attempt intimate conversations that risk embarrassment, emotional nakedness, and extreme vulnerability?

The bottom line of risk in a romantic relationship is this: If we don't venture into realms of reflection and action that push our limits and challenge our existing vision of what life is all about, we remain forever prisoners of our existing habits and boundaries of experience.

Risk is the key to growth. If risk generates a twinge of fear inside us, then our challenge is to deal with the fear, not to reject the risk. Let me share with you some important words of wisdom from a spiritual teacher who recently passed away. On several occasions, I had very deep conversations with this man whose writings contain a very important perspective on things spiritual and things sexual as well, since he was a great believer in the transcendent powers of sexual relating. I'm speaking of the Indian teacher Bhagwan Shree Rajneesh, and am quoting now from his *Book of the Secrets*, volume four:

> It is said that one who is in fear cannot love, nor reach Godhood. But how is one to get rid of fear? The question is not of getting rid of anything. The question is only of understanding. Understand fear, what it is. Don't try to get rid of it, because the moment you start trying to get rid of anything, you are not ready to understand it—because the mind which thinks to get rid of is already closed. It cannot contemplate quietly; it has already decided. If you have fear, then accept it as part of your being. If you can accept it, it has disappeared already. Through acceptance, fear disappears; through denial, fear increases. A miracle happens when you accept a truth. The very acceptance changes you. You accept yourself—and through this acceptance, love arises. It fills your being. You are not afraid of fear, you are not trying to get rid of it. Simply it disappears when accepted. Accept your authentic being with all its anxieties and you will be transformed.

As a therapist, much of my work over the years has been to help clients accept their fears so that they can risk knowing themselves, accepting themselves, and loving others. Bhagwan Shree Rajneesh spoke important words that certainly ring true about accepting fear. But how do we actually manage to carry through with his words of wisdom?

What I want to offer you is a short set of pragmatic experiential steps that you can readily apply to your own intimate relating in order to help you face anxiety-provoking sexual situations in such a way as to transcend your fears progressively and thus allow more honest relating to take place.

FEAR REDUCTION ONE:
Make Your Breathing Most Important

When you are in an intimate situation that makes you feel nervous, remember that your breathing is where fear grips you. If you can focus your attention on your breathing, your power of attention will spontaneously generate a movement toward emotional expression and ensuing relaxation in your breathing muscles. This is one of the great tricks to learn in life—that your power of attention is a palpable force that you can use to generate positive changes inside you. In this case, as your breathing calms down and deepens, you will feel yourself being liberated from emotional constrictions that inhibit deep conversational intimacy with your lover.

FEAR REDUCTION TWO:
You Don't Have to Do Anything

When we become anxious in an intimate situation, when our voices tighten up and our breathing gets shallow, we usually feel a pressure to do something to escape from the tense situation. We tend to slip into shallow verbal behavior and mental/emotional patterns that only worsen the tension by exacerbating our loss of heart contact right when we urgently need that deep level of honesty with our lover.

The trick at this point is to realize that the best move is very often to make no move at all. Instead of trying to escape the situation, it is vastly more productive to relax right in the middle of the situation, so that insightful self-observations can be made. Especially in terms of fear reduction, it is important to realize that the encounter is not a life-or-death situation. Instead, it is a new chance to see clearly why we become tense and afraid, and, through seeing the truth, to grow in the process.

FEAR REDUCTION THREE:
Perceptual Shifting

As we are exploring on many fronts in this book, the process of genuine spiritual growth involves the conscious act of seeing ourselves and our lover with more honesty and clarity. This process of acceptant seeing requires that we learn to become temporarily quiet and calm, and willing to risk a new realization in the present moment.

The trick of moving beyond conversational nervousness in an intimate situation is to remain silent long enough to feel a connection with our emotions before saying anything further. Like Matt, most of us tend to be afraid of silence when we are with someone. We must discipline ourselves to experience this silence deeply enough so that when we reengage our vocal apparatus, we speak not only at thinking levels but at heart levels, as well.

The vehicle that both therapists and spiritual teachers alike use as the primary way for attaining this essential silence, calmness, and self-awareness needed for self-seeing and personal growth is what we call "perceptual shifting." This technique involves shifting your focus of attention away from the habitual thought flows and conditioned reflexes that usually dominate an encounter, and focusing instead on the perceptual reality of your own presence—your breathing and physical body, and the immediate experiences coming to you through your senses that bring you a direct awareness of the person you are with.

In reality, the simple and yet infinitely subtle act of learning to shift your attention to your experience of breathing your next breath has been the primary spiritual technique employed by advanced men and women throughout the world. In this primal act of conscious mental shifting, we are able to move beyond our past, our conditioned reactions, and into position for direct encounter with the present moment.

Then, after establishing a deep awareness of your breathing, the next phase of perceptual shifting is to expand your awareness of your breathing so that you are aware of your whole body at once, as a vital physical presence. Feel gravity pulling on every muscle, for instance. Feel your heartbeat or pulse throughout your body. Know your self as a living entity in the present moment.

Beyond this physiological dimension of self-awareness, your five senses are also actively sampling the environment, putting you in intimate sensory contact with the person with whom you are sharing space. This sensory awareness of sharing actual three-dimensional space with your lover is what makes true intimacy in a sexual relationship come alive.

FEAR REDUCTION FOUR:
Let Your Heart Speak

Once you have made the first three steps I just outlined (and will explore with you in more depth in later chapters), you are in the position to speak to your lover in a new way, with your whole being rather than just through your pro-grammed "head trip" conversational patterns. If you are in tune with your breathing and your heartbeat in the present moment, you are by definition in tune with your heart feel-ings. So when you speak, you will naturally communicate deeper feelings and thoughts. Your anxiety will be lower, so you can risk being more vulnerable.

"Clancy scared me to death, that's the truth of the matter," Matt confessed one day. "She was wanting to see parts of me that I thought would make her reject me instantly. I had to overcome a ton of fear before I could even manage to tell her that she scared me. But once I did tell her she scared me, wow, I felt a sudden release inside me, and everything was different. I broke out laughing, that's what I did. My fear was so stupid. After all, this was a woman who really loved me, not someone out to use my confessions against me. That was just old family paranoia. I realized I was going to have to learn how to separate myself from my past if I was going to be able to keep this woman."

I suggest that you take time to memorize these four fear-reduction steps to expanding conversational intimacies be-fore we move on. Look back over them now if you want, so that your memory has them stored and ready to use in your next intimate conversation.

Don't Judge Your Voice

One of the curious universal tendencies in our present culture is that of rejecting one's own voice when it is played
back on a tape recorder. Very few people like the sound of
their own voice when heard as other people hear it. We tend
to judge ourselves terribly negatively in this regard. We
hear only the tensions, the brittleness, the phoniness, the
weakness in our voice—those qualities we are most afraid
are really true about us.

The rock-bottom reality is that very few contemporary
Americans have genuine voices. Most of us employ habitual
phony intonations when we speak. I have noticed a great
difference, for instance, between the emotional vulnerability
and honesty in the voices of people in my own community
and the voices of people in communities of primitive tribes
I have lived with while doing anthropological research some
years back in Mexico, Guatemala, and southern Africa. Most
of the people in these Third World communities have reso-
nant, honest voices that are a pleasure to listen to. Most of
us are just the opposite, and therefore we hate to hear our
own voices.

Be this as it may, if we reject our own voices because of
how bothersome they might be to listen to, we are rejecting
our very own selves. And this act of self-denial is vastly more
damaging to us than accepting that our voices are uptight
and a bit forced or even downright phony much of the
time. We simply must accept ourselves. This is the primal
necessity, as I have said already, for spiritual as well as psychological growth.

What an amazing step it is in therapy when a client finally
realizes that instant self-obliteration will not necessarily occur if the client says to him- or herself, "I realize I'm an

emotional wreck compared with how I could be without all my inhibitions. But I accept myself just as I am, anyway."

Jesus was making this same point when He said, "Judge not, lest ye be judged." If we judge ourselves as no good, everyone around us will pick up on this attitude and think we're no good, too. But if we accept ourselves, people around us will tend to accept us. This is one of the most powerful laws of interpersonal relating.

Pause a bit and reflect on your relationship with your own voice. How do you sound on a tape recorder? How do you sound to people listening to you? And can you accept that this is you now, and that it's okay?

Vocal Awakening

If making vocal contact with your lover at heart levels is indeed a problem for you, what concrete steps can you take, beyond the four fear-reduction suggestions I made a few pages ago, to improve your conversational honesty and intimacy?

Simple observation of your existing habits for at least a week is highly recommended before you try to make any alterations in your vocal relating. Just see what you say and how well you listen when next with your lover. Observe yourself in action.

As a general guideline, check out the following key features of your conversational habits:

1. Are you the dominant talker in your sexual relationship?
2. Is your voice honest or phony when you talk?

3. Do you speak of things that are close to your heart, or do you keep the conversation at shallow levels?
4. Do you like the sound of your own voice?
5. Are you aware of your breathing while talking?
6. Is there an underlying anxiety in your voice?
7. Can you speak of your feelings of vulnerability to your lover?
8. Do you hear all the emotional innuendos of your friend's voice, or do you tend to listen very poorly to your lover's emotional undertones while conversing?
9. Do you accept the voice of your lover, or are you judging?
10. Can you tell your lover honestly when you feel nervous, upset, angry, or depressed, or do you hide your negative feelings?

Emotional-Release Vocal Exercises

The emotional-release tradition of bioenergetics and Reichian therapy is an excellent personal-growth tradition begun by Wilhelm Reich some fifty years ago. He was a true pioneer in modern psychology who risked and sacrificed a great deal professionally in order to gaze as deeply as he could into the ways in which our emotional conditionings as children inhibit our ability to have heart contact as adults. Let me share with you two simple and yet powerful exercises from this emotional-release approach to personal growth.

Relax That Jaw Muscle!

When we are forced to inhibit our emotions, we unconsciously learn to hold our jaw muscle tight so that spontaneous outbursts won't be able to escape from our mouths
and get us into trouble. People with tense voices invariably
have tight jaw muscles, and tense tongue and larynx muscles, too, since they are so intimately related. Once you
learn to detect the tension in this throat region of your
body and to relax it consciously, your voice can in fact
become remarkably more relaxed, enjoyable, expressive,
and impressive.

The key to this relaxation of jaw and tongue is to let the
upper and lower teeth part just slightly instead of holding
them clenched against each other. It's downright saddening
to observe that the large majority of people in line at the
grocery store or at work habitually hold their jaws tightly
shut in pointless contraction when not talking. To break
this habit is not only to open your oral passage but to relax
your heart, and also to relax and open sexually. Fear that is
held chronically in the vocal apparatus generalizes to the
whole body, as recent physiological research has documented. And to make the conscious act of dropping the jaw
so the teeth are just slightly apart and the jaw and tongue
muscles relaxed is to do something extremely helpful and
pleasurable to yourself.

Notice your state of tension or relaxation in your throat
right now . . . experiment with different ways to relax this
region of your body . . . feel how your entire breathing
relaxes and feels better when you are consciously relaxing
your jaw, tongue, and throat regions.

VOCAL RELEASE TWO:
Saying "Blaahhhh!" to the World

As children, almost all of us were forced to inhibit certain feelings. To indulge consciously in these vocalizations as adults can be an instant liberation. The key expression is this: Open your mouth, stick out your tongue, and let a beautiful "Blaahhhh!" come out of you, expressing the feeling of being fed up with everything around you, especially all the emotional tensions in your body from childhood programmings.

As an adult, you can bring immediate release simply by doing this exercise once an hour, probably when no one is watching you, or with someone who has read this book and appreciates the sentiment. In intimacy workshops, we walk around in a loose circle and "Blaahh!" everyone we encounter, letting other people see us in this forbidden mood—it's great fun!

See what experience comes to you if you say "Blaahhhh!" several times . . . be open to a vocal rush of emotions that might like to rise up from your depths and be expressed.

Speaking Words of Love

Sexual arousal itself has a dramatic effect on our voices if we are open enough to allow it. Our vocal quality becomes more and more relaxed and hoarse, for instance, as we surrender to the progression toward deep orgasmic union with our lover. Instead of talking theoretical talk or shoptalk, we find words becoming less and less important. Primal sounds instead begin to rise up inside us, begging for expression in groans and cries of sexual pleasure and abandon.

Conversely, when a person's voice is chronically tight, when sounds are inhibited or faked, the deeper orgasm experience is blocked. Men can actually reach the point of ejaculation without surrendering to their primal vocal expressions. With jaws tight and teeth clenched, many men go about lovemaking as if it was a tense battle or task, rather than tapping into the true magic of spontaneous orgasm.

Most women find it almost impossible to have full orgasm unless they relax their jaw muscles and let go of their habitual vocal tensions for at least long enough to reach orgasm. In later chapters we will speak much more of the vocal dimension of orgasm, where verbal communion falls away and the more instinctive powers of sexual merging take over.

There is a definite progression to an intimate conversation that begins as light talking between two people who are sexually attracted to each other, and then deepens step by step, first into verbal intimacy, then into physical intimacy, and then hopefully into mystic union. You can begin to observe for yourself how you personally progress through different phases of verbal intercourse while making love.

Let me ask you a few more specific questions regarding your vocal habits, questions to ponder in regard to past sexual encounters, and also to hold in mind the next time you find yourself approaching lovemaking:

1. Do you tend to talk a lot when becoming sexually excited, or do you easily manage to let conversational relating drop off so that you can get swept away into nonverbal levels of sexual intercourse?

2. Do you express your growing sexual passions with the primal animal sounds of agony and ecstasy, or do you

habitually block these sounds from coming out of your mouth?

3. Are you open to let your lover be spontaneously vocal while making love?

4. After making love, do you feel relaxed and satisfied in your vocal apparatus (your breathing muscles, your vocal cords, your jaw and tongue muscles), or do you feel more tense than before sexual intercourse?

5. After making love, do you remain silent and enjoy the nonverbal depths of sharing, or do you immediately start talking again?

We should always hold in mind that all the utterances we make while having sexual intercourse are definite communications. Just because, as orgasm approaches, we might no longer be using cogent words to express our feelings, we are still revealing to our lover how we are responding to being intimate with them in that moment. Each of us by nature has an instinctive set of sounds that come out of us spontaneously when we let them while making love. To get to know more clearly what our lover is actually expressing with his or her gutteral sounds and sentence fragments is very important to a fulfilling sexual relationship.

I remember early in my sexual adventures a particular experience where my lover and I were so deeply into our shared wild beastly sexual feelings that for the first time I lost myself completely to the merging of my body with that of another person. Then suddenly, under me, I heard this passionate voice crying out to me in a great wailing moan, "No, no, no!" She meant that she was ready to surrender to the total obliteration of ego that orgasm temporarily brings. But I took her words at face value and pulled back, much to her dismay. Obviously, I didn't understand what she was saying with her words.

We often say many things while making love that, taken at face value, or repeated at the bridge club, would seem very strange indeed. "Words come out of my mouth," a client once told me, "that are shockingly vulgar, that I never use in everyday conversation—but that are absolutely the only words that exactly express my feelings at that moment. At first, I used to shock myself, and tried to block such wild pornographic outbursts. But as the years have gone by, I've learned that I can't really have the sexual experience I hunger for unless I let my voice be completely free to say anything at all, even the grossest obscenities. And if my lover can't take me just as I am, then that's just too bad for him."

The Truth Will Out

In similar manner, even long before we reach the hot passions of full-blown sexual intercourse, we often find ourselves saying things to our lover that surprise us, as we express thoughts that we have never quite even managed to say to ourselves before.

Often we think that in order to speak the truth to someone, we must first of all have established the truth in our own minds. This is to overlook completely a primary dynamic and magic of vocal intercourse, however. Conversations between intimates are, after all, not based primarily on the cursory exchange of known data and established attitudes. Instead, deep communion at vocal levels is a process whereby we risk talking right at the cutting edge of our present level of realization.

My understanding of true friendship is this—that on all levels it provides us with an essential vehicle for exploring our personal capacity to see reality more clearly. When we are talking with our lover, for instance, we are not just speaking of things we know perfectly well. We are using the experience of talking in order to expand our own understanding of who we are and what life is all about.

In short, in the process of speaking to our lover, we can suddenly find ourselves speaking deeper truths than we have ever encountered before. We discover what is true for ourselves by exploring a spontaneous flow of thoughts with someone who listens to us in an acceptant, loving, and adventuresome spirit.

In this way, conversations become an extremely exciting, creative process that generates continual self-discovery and at the same time shares this discovery with someone we love. This is true intimacy! When someone is looking intently into his or her own experience of life, and in the process of expressing his or her feelings and thoughts discovering a deeper level of understanding of the topic under discussion, then this conversation is blessed.

This sharing of our spontaneous thoughts and feelings, realizations and intimations is one of the greatest gifts we can give to someone we love. Likewise, one of the greatest gifts we can give to someone we love is to listen in such a way as to encourage our friend's own process of self-discovery.

For most of us, however, this way of listening and talking does not come easily. We must consciously work to discipline ourselves in certain ways, so that a creative, inspired flow of communication can be opened between us.

Let me offer you a set of guidelines showing what you can do to encourage your lover to speak from the heart, to make new discoveries while talking to you:

1. Listen to the tone of your lover's voice and not just to the ideas being expressed.

2. Listen without interrupting for good lengths of time, so that you allow your friend the space to express something deep from the heart.
3. Listen without thinking of anything to say in response.
4. Listen without judging.
5. Discipline yourself never to talk more than you listen in a relationship, or even in a casual conversation with a stranger.
6. See whether you can stay aware of your breathing throughout, and also of your heart region in your body, so that your focus of attention is deep down instead of just up in the head.
7. Likewise discipline yourself so that when you are with your lover, you take regular breaks from conversing, allowing silence to have equal time in your relationship. Learn to be quiet together, to tune in to your bodies and get out of your minds for regular intervals.

These are simple and yet potent suggestions. They take time to master, so don't judge yourself for falling short of the ultimate sense of balance in conversational relating. Your challenge is to pay attention regularly to these dimensions of vocal intercourse, so that your power of attention can act to stimulate spontaneous corrections in your earlier programming and liberate you from inhibitions that directly interfere with your sexual communion with your lover.

Perhaps you might enjoy another "memory expedition" at this point, in which you relax, put the book aside after reading this paragraph, and drift back to the last times you have made love, remembering many moments in the entire progression toward orgasm. In light of what we have been exploring in this chapter, what do you observe regarding your level of vocal intercourse with your lover?

4
Risking Visual Intercourse

Sharon was by nature a very shy girl. Her shyness was compounded by the fact that she was quite lovely, with a head of wild blond hair and blue eyes. Her big brothers often made fun of her, which made things worse. And puberty was an excruciatingly painful ordeal for her; her body blossomed and the boys and grown men alike were all ogling her. So she just shut everyone out by never returning passionate glances at all. When she grew up, she lived within her own inner worlds and seldom let anyone see her true feelings. Even when she got married, she was afraid to let her husband see the visual depths of her soul, especially in the heat of passion. As a result, she felt hidden, isolated, unable to reveal to anyone her innermost feelings. Her potential for experiencing true spiritual intimacy was thus directly blocked.

Ancient philosophical wisdom from all the world traditions teaches as one of its primary theses the spiritual truth that "the eyes are the windows of the soul." Just a moment ago, as if to highlight this theme, my two-year-old son came running into my writing room with his eyes ablaze with feelings that he can't even express in words yet. What power there is in a glance!

We were all once upon a time, just like my son, extremely vulnerable visual beings. We spontaneously trusted the world around us without question. We had no fear of facing reality head-on. We lived constantly within the perceptual intensity of direct, intuitive intercourse with life itself.

I have spoken of this theme in one of my earlier books, *The Visual Handbook*: "When we were very young, our eyes functioned in a state of relative bliss. They were free to look wherever they wanted, to explore the visual world without control or inhibitions. A natural spontaneity existed visually, a quality that gave basic vitality and health to the eyes. Seeing was a pleasure, the eyes remained relaxed, active, full of curiosity and joy."

Then for many of us came embarrassing and bashful feelings, and often downright negative visual encounters with people around us. Step by step, we lost our readiness to let just anyone gaze into the depths of our souls in spontaneous visual intercourse. We developed ways of avoiding the risk of being visually abused or embarrassed. Like Sharon, each of us came to learn the hard way that sometimes the outside world can't be trusted to see directly into our souls. Sometimes people abuse us when we are open and vulnerable. Sometimes it is dangerous to expose our inner feelings by flashing completely revealing glances into someone else's eyes.

The visual-avoidance patterns young people learn to develop include both an obvious averting of the eyes to dodge the glances of other people and also a more complex mental trick of looking into someone's eyes but keeping an invisible barrier up to hide our spiritual and sexual selves. People can stare into our eyes but, in Wilhelm Reich's psychological terminology, we have become "armored" inside, protected by an interior mental membrane through which other people's glances cannot penetrate to our interior realms of being.

It should be pointed out that in many instances, a youngster's fear of being seen is not a reaction to actual threats from the outside world. Instead, this visual veiling of one's feelings can develop purely out of a youngster's budding sense of self-awareness, where natural feelings of bashfulness make one extremely shy about being seen at all. My youngest son, for instance, has already gone through his first short period of bashfulness just a few months ago, only to emerge quickly out of that first sense of shy self-awareness into his presently extroverted phase. I know from experience, however, that he will have several similar bouts of visual bashfulness before he hits puberty. And when he becomes a teenager, this sense of shyness and aversion to direct visual intercourse will rise up again, sometimes extremely painfully from an emotional point of view.

What in fact is happening when someone feels bashful at the visual level of intercourse? Why is it sometimes so difficult to look our lover in the eyes, to see and be seen instantly and to our depths?

This question has been discussed since the beginnings of recorded history. It is obvious that our underlying sense of communion with the world around us depends on how we habitually establish our visual interaction with people. And the key point psychologically is this—that the act of perception always involves both our sensing of the outside world and, at the same time, our sensing of our own inner presence. The combination of inner and outer, of object and subject, is what makes awareness function.

The true challenge of human beings is in fact to maintain both inner and outer awareness at the same time. When there is an equal balance in our consciousness of object and subject, of outer and inner, of other and self, then we are in true spiritual communion with the world around us, and experience a union of self and other.

This is ideally what happens on all levels during sexual intercourse, where we are aware equally of our inner sexual presence and the sexual presence of our lover. This intense communion can also happen with sometimes equal intensity quite outside an overt sexual encounter.

"I flew over to Zurich for a meeting," an executive friend of mine confessed to me recently, "and caught the shuttle train from the airport into town. I was in a curious mood, feeling somehow full and content inside myself. Without thinking, I raised my eyes and found myself looking directly into those of a woman across from me. She had the most intensely beautiful eyes I had ever seen. And the impact of her visual contact felt like an actual explosion inside me, as if I'd been struck instantly to the quick. When the doors of the train opened, we hardly realized the ride was over. It was as if we were inside each other, lost in each other, in some world that is totally different from regular life. Then suddenly, she turned and walked away. I never saw her again, but I'll always have her in my heart. It's like I lived with her for years instead of moments."

Love at first sight is a magical happening. We have all experienced such intense visual encounters that struck us to the quick instantly and lingered in our hearts long after. For some people, such short visual encounters are the true highlights of their romantic lives.

Why don't you take a few moments to look back into your own past, and remember visual encounters where you were instantly penetrated by the visual presence of a stranger. Relive the intensity of this eye-to-eye nakedness and intimacy with a stranger you let touch your very soul.

Hold on to Your Spiritual Hat

As we are seeing step by step, sexual and spiritual intimacy are both based on our ability to remain sensitive and vulnerable, in tune with our own inner presence, while also opening our personal worlds to welcome another being into our bubble of awareness. Each new time we open up to our lover, each time we shed clothes and superficial facades and encounter each other directly, it is only natural to feel a temporary sense of bashfulness. This bashfulness is a response of our inner self as it becomes suddenly acutely aware of its own deeper mysteries and secrets. Right at this point, it is indeed scary to let someone see into our inner realms of being.

People who don't feel this, who have buried their natural shyness, who hold their bashful feelings under habitual control, remain closed off to the deeper levels of spiritual intimacy. They might be able to brazenly stare their lóver in the eye while stripping, and feel no shyness at all in the face of their lover's nakedness. But if they are hardened to their spontaneous feelings of awe and bashfulness, they will lack what it takes for attaining full sexual communion.

This is one half of the picture—that visual shyness is healthy and to be encouraged. However, there also comes the time in making love when passion should overwhelm shyness, where we burst beyond our bashful feelings and become totally open and vulnerable and unafraid. We will see in later chapters that as we advance toward orgasm, we become filled with a powerful sexual energy that blasts us free from all our ego inhibitions, propelling us into purely spontaneous interactions with our lover.

Making love is without doubt a series of progressive shifts of consciousness as we play out the complex and yet perfectly natural and spontaneous dance that takes us deeper and deeper into realms of spiritual encounter and sexual surrender. The challenge of sexual fulfillment is learning how to move through the various steps of lovemaking without getting hung up in and unable to let go of one of the steps.

Many people are without doubt hung up at the visual level of intercourse, so seriously contracted against visual intimacy that they habitually and mostly unconsciously keep their visual souls veiled, armored, unavailable for communion with their lover. My client Sharon, as we have seen, was such an extreme case. As she was growing up and moving through puberty, she found that wherever she went, men around were sending out messages of overt sexual interest through their own glances, which scared her. She came to feel that in a single glance, a man could penetrate, almost sexually violate her.

"Boys in school would flash me a hot look and it was like they instantly were inside me. Long before I really knew all about how a man penetrates a woman, I felt this feeling through my eyes. And I felt as if something terrible had happened to me. Of course, it didn't help that my mother was rigid sexually, maybe if I hadn't picked up my mother's fears of sexuality, I would have enjoyed the boys shooting visual semen in my direction. But I was afraid of sex, deathly afraid for no reason at all except that my mother was afraid of it. And when men started nailing me with looks that made me want just to pass out, I learned how to go blank instantly internally. I just went away. And even now ten years later, I'm still afraid, even when Jack and I are doing it. I close my eyes and then everything's okay. But I can't really meet those beautiful brown eyes of his when he's inside me. When I do, it's as if my own inner self gets wiped out instantly. I feel him taking over my soul and then I just pass out, I close my eyes and retreat deep inside me until I can find myself again."

Sexual Masters

If we do find ourselves overly shy visually, unable to really open up and plunge into the mysteries of visual intercourse with our lover, and unable to share even quick intimate glances with other people around us, what can we do to overcome this ingrained inhibition?

As we saw earlier, each new step we advance into sexual intimacy can generate new feelings of anxiety inside us, and make us contract. When we open ourselves up another notch, we always risk, and this risking behavior carries with it fear of exposure, of vulnerability.

First of all, the same basic lessons that we learned for expanding verbal intimacy apply equally well to visual intercourse. Very often, we find ourselves engaging in visual intercourse right at the same time that we're conversing with our lover. Sometimes the visual communion becomes so intense that words fall away. It is a fairly reasonable assumption to say that true visual intercourse is of a higher level of intensity than verbal intercourse. A flow of words keeps us locked into a linear, rational sense of time and meaning. The visual experience transports us away from past-future thinking and into the timelessness of the eternal present moment. This is why so many people fixate upon talking and avoid deep visual intercourse at least early in a sexual encounter, as a way to sidestep an intensity that scares them.

Ideally, of course, we can talk and look into each other's eyes at the same time, merging the two realms of consciousness and encounter into one. In fact, it is almost always prolonged visual contact while talking that suddenly plunges verbal intercourse into deeper realms of sharing. A very magical thing happens: When eyes meet and souls come together in the flash of a passionate glance, the thinking function of the mind spontaneously expands to include the more intuitive dimensions of human consciousness. Right at this point, the person speaking will start expressing ideas that are new, creative, self-revelatory.

For this to happen, there must be at the same time a deep awareness of one's own center, and a deep awareness of one's lover's center. To lose one's own center during verbal and visual intercourse means to drift into relative unconsciousness. To fixate too much on one's own inner center means to avoid contact with one's lover. There must be a finely balanced attunement of consciousness in order to maintain communion.

At each new stage of sexual relating, it is essential to learn how to establish and maintain this crucial balance. Furthermore, at each new stage, we must surrender the level of consciousness of the last stage, so that the new phase can explode into being. Throughout, we must hold our own inner sense of balance like masters if we are to move through the entire process without dropping out of the spiritual dimensions of sexual union.

However, to be a master at making love does not mean

to become a control freak, dominating and directing the show. There is nothing more boring in bed than someone who has mastered all the techniques of intercourse and tries to force the flow of sexual communion.

The true master of love is the one who simply remains centered and conscious, and surrenders to the purely spontaneous instinctual energies that rise up and effortlessly orchestrate the sexual encounter. Egowise, there is in truth nothing to do in order to achieve sexual union. We have only to relax into the natural sequence of biological events and let the sexual energies carry us away. It is only when our inhibitions and conditioned contractions interfere with the flow, when we react with anxiety and then upset our delicate inner balance, that we lose the magic of transpersonal union.

Our primary aim in making love is therefore to master the fine art of remaining spontaneous, vulnerable, balanced, and conscious while allowing our instinctive spiritual powers of sexual love to possess us in complete abandon. When this state of consciousness is reached while making love, the inflow of spiritual overtones to sexual love comes rushing into us, bringing the transpersonal experience of mystic union for which we hunger.

Inner Balance During Visual Intercourse

In order to attain and maintain this state of spontaneous participation in the greater powers of mystic relating, it is required that we learn how to hold our sense of balance between inner and outer focus of attention all during lovemaking. Let me share with you the same basic balancing techniques that I taught Sharon for overcoming her visual inhibitions, so that you can apply these in your own intimate situations where needed.

As the first essential step, I asked Sharon simply to observe for a couple of weeks what actually happens to her visually when relating intimately. "It seems to be always the same," she told me afterward. "Whenever I'm feeling deep emotions inside me while talking to someone, and glance into their eyes, my breathing just freezes. My body acts like a robot. I can't stop it, it just happens. At the same instant, I feel a constriction in my throat, and a tensing in my stomach. All this makes me feel both dizzy and uncomfortable. Usually I drop the visual relating completely and focus on the conversation. If I try to maintain the eye contact, I feel a flush of embarrassment—and phase out and lose my train of thought completely. The more intimate, and especially sexual, I feel with someone, the more I get hit with this pattern. I'll be right in the middle of a conversation with someone I want to get to know better, and then somehow everything suddenly drops down to a deeper level, a more intense feeling, and I just blow my cool. Somehow I feel threatened whenever sexual energies rise up. Instead of feeling good inside my body, I'm suddenly feeling bad."

Sharon is describing a typically painful anxiety attack. In essence, her uncertain ego identity feels in danger of being swamped by the presence of the other person. In Michael Hutchison's new book, *The Anatomy of Sex and Power*, philosopher Murray Davis explains how, during intense sexual relating, a person's self-image is no longer experienced as stable and unchanging. "The self seems to become more malleable, more open to alteration, during sexual arousal. . . . The psychological energy that normally sustains identity boundaries is suspended. . . . By turning off the defenses that normally preserve the integrity of the identity, sexual arousal temporarily opens the identity to essential change."

Psychologically, and spiritually as well, our basic fear in becoming more intimate is the fear of undergoing "essential change" in our sense of who we are. This is certainly part of the dynamic of bashfulness. The fear is a realistic one, of course, because the power of sexual energies rushing into our bodies is most definitely strong enough to provoke expansions of consciousness that could forever alter our limited concepts of who we are and what life is all about.

The old restricted ego structure we have developed must always undergo a death-rebirth experience if we are to grow spiritually. This is what Jesus seems to have been talking about at more subtle levels when he spoke of becoming born again in the spirit: We must let go of our ego concept of who we are if we are to experience directly our infinite spiritual identity.

So Sharon's fear response to visual intercourse, to sharing her soul with another person and momentarily being transported through visual intercourse into mystic realms of transcendence, was in a sense a completely valid fear. She is an extremely mystic person, very sensitive to the spiritual presence of people she meets—and therefore very bashful.

"I don't feel that I've wasted all these years while being bashful," she told me toward the end of our therapy work together. "I had to get to know myself in a lot of ways before I could share my feelings with other people. And I can see that I'm going to spend the rest of my life in the process of expanding more and more, and that makes life such a rich experience."

The question we need to look at directly is this: How do

we best lead ourselves beyond the reactive fears against visual intercourse, so that we can continue in our lifelong journey toward deeper and deeper relating?

There is only one direct antidote that I have found for quieting the fear reaction caused by a deepening of visual intimacy in an encounter. Once again, the solution has to do with the breath factor. If consciousness can be directed to the breathing right when the breathing becomes uptight with apprehension, then the breathing will calm down, the conversation can continue, and intimate eye contact can remain in action, too.

When I first suggested to Sharon that she begin to learn to stay aware of her breathing while talking and meeting someone's eyes, she said, "But that's impossible. I'm so caught up in the words and the eyes and everything else that I don't have any attention left over for my breathing."

In practice, as she found out, this isn't necessarily the case. It's quite possible to learn how to be aware of one's breathing as a central experience, and to expand one's awareness to include virtually an infinity of external happenings and inner thought flows. The heart of all true spiritual paths is, in fact, the development of this ability to expand one's conscious experience out from the core of one's being, infinitely in all directions. Our sexual-intimacy application of this basic spiritual technique is just one dimension of the entire process, as we will see in later chapters.

In fact, what Sharon was trying to communicate to me, as we found out through more conversation, was that when fear hits her nervous system, her overall consciousness suddenly contracts, making it extremely hard right at that moment for her to be aware of anything at all. She was relinquishing her inner sense of self-awareness in order to make contact with another person, instead of holding on to her own inner center as primary, and expanding out from that inner center.

The psychological requirements for creating a spiritually-passionate conversation are that (a) we remain aware of our own inner center through being aware of our breathing and whole-body experience, while (b) we expand our awareness to include our perceptual contacts with the person to whom we are talking, while (c) we participate in the verbal flow of ideas being exchanged.

The key point that my colleagues and I have discovered through repeated observations in therapy work, and that spiritual masters have known for at least five thousand years, is that in order to attain this multidimensional quality in a conversation, we must make breath awareness primary, and expand out from this inner core of awareness, rather than trying to do it the other way around. "But that means that I'd have to drop out of the conversation in order to find my breathing," Sharon complained, "and if I do that, I'll lose whatever intimacy already exists between me and my friend."

This is not what usually happens, however. Usually, moments of silence deepen a conversation rather than ruin it. My suggestion to Sharon, and to you, as well, if this approach to intimacy is appealing, is as follows:

1. Definitely fall silent when you lose your sense of inner centeredness.
2. Let your friend continue talking or fall silent with you.
3. Consciously drop your attention down into your breathing.
4. Regain contact with your emotions and your physical presence in the present moment, and allow these emotions to be visible.

This recentering process takes only a few breaths to accomplish after you have mastered it. And immediately after you have performed this shifting of your attention, you will find that suddenly your bubble of awareness expands again, you are present again, and ready to expand another notch to include your friend with you in your bubble of consciousness.

Let me show in a bit more detail what actually happens when you consciously redirect your attention to your breathing and whole-body presence. In practice, most conversations tend to be head trips, where intellectual functions of consciousness overwhelm emotional, physical, and spiritual dimensions of awareness. Specifically, we tend to lose awareness of our heart region when we talk. This directly short-circuits intimate sharing. By shifting our attention to the region of our chest, which is where not only the lungs but also the heart are to be found, we consciously reestablish connection with our emotional center down in our torso.

Another vital benefit of shifting to an awareness of our breathing is that this shift brings us instantly into the present moment. Remember that thoughts are past-future functions in our time orientation. Breathing is a purely present-moment happening. You can see what I mean for yourself as you continue reading these words—by observing what happens inside you if you tune into your own breathing experience even as you are reading . . . feel the air rushing in and out through your nose with every new inhale and exhale . . . experience the actual sensations in your chest and belly as your muscles expand to let air rush into your lungs with every new inhale . . . and contract to push the air out with every new exhale . . . expand your awareness to include whatever emotions are present in your body as you breathe and read . . . and feel the beautiful whole-body experience of being involved with words and thinking in your

head . . . and at the same time being aware of your breathing
. . . your whole body here in the eternal present moment . . .
and your emotions . . . all at the same time . . . in this
expanded state of awareness into which you have just effortlessly shifted yourself.

The Primal "In and Out"

In early research I did for the National Institutes of Health,
my colleagues and I showed how fear is definitely a function
of the inhale reflex. This means that when we are suddenly
frightened, we reflexively inhale, unless the fear is so great
that our breathing is completely frozen in our chests. Likewise, we found in our research that excitement stimulates
the inhale reflex.

You almost certainly know these basic human reflexes
from personal experience. Notice, when you next find yourself in an intimate conversation, whether the following
breath experience happens to you: As you become more
passionate, as intimacies deepen, as intensities and quite
possibly uncertainties well up inside you, does your breathing tend to get stuck on the inhale? Do you hold yourself
full of air, and thus make yourself dizzy?

The word *inspiration* often best describes the feelings inside the chests of two people involved in passionate verbal
and visual intercourse. *Inspiration* is a word drawn from
the Greek *inspire*, which means to expand or fill up, and
secondarily to inhale.

Especially during intense visual intercourse, where rising
passions scare us a bit with their intensity, we tend to hold
our breath in general. When we hold our breath, oxygen

quickly drops in the bloodstream, and thus in the brain, while carbon dioxide builds up. The result is a temporary imbalance in the basic biochemical functioning of the brain. This is primarily why people afraid of visual intercourse feel anxious and dizzy—they are starving themselves of oxygen and putting their entire nervous system into a panic.

When I explained this to Sharon, she could see much more clearly why she tended to become so strange during intense visual intercourse. And she told me a couple of weeks later, "I actually had to burst right out laughing at myself when I caught myself doing just that when talking with Ralph. I caught myself not breathing! And you were right— I was all puffed up like a balloon, with my exhale frozen. And as soon as I noticed it, everything changed, I was breathing again."

Gary Zukav has pointed out in *The Dancing Wu Li Masters,* in which he has integrated brand-new findings of physics with the ancient wisdom of the Taoist spiritual masters of China, that the entire universe seems to be built upon the theme of a proverbial "in-out" movement. The primary sine wave of the universe vacillates regularly and with perfect balance between an extreme high point and an extreme low point, and so does our breathing, as we inhale up, and then exhale down, over and over again, as the primary happening of every moment of our long lives. This movement of air rushing in, then air rushing out, then air rushing in again defines our entire existence in life from the cradle to the grave.

Likewise of course in the sexual act, this "in-out" format defines the basic thrust of intercourse. Notice next time you are making love how your breathing and your pelvic movements tend to move in synchronistic harmony.

In conversation, this rhythmic pattern must be maintained, as well, for a balanced relationship to ensue. First one person talks and the other listens. Then hopefully the first person is quiet and receptive so that the other person can discharge, send out, broadcast.

Even in visual intercourse, this is an essential dynamic of intimate balance: Eyes can be powerful and projecting, and also soft and receiving. There is nothing more bothersome than someone who is in the "on" position all the time with his or her eyes, constantly blasting you with his or her presence, and never softening and becoming vulnerable so that you can send out your own visual presence and touch the depths of his or her soul.

I remember, a dozen years ago when I was doing anthropological research high in the mountains of western Mexico, talking with a Huichole Indian *brujo* (wise man) about visual intercourse. This man had eyes like I have never seen since, sometimes sharp as a falcon's, penetrating instantly to the heart, but instantly able to shift, to turn off this remarkable visual presence, and become like a vast loving pool of compassion, into which I would feel myself being absorbed with zero resistance as I met his eyes with my own presence.

"Do you think there's actually a force, a detectable energy that radiates from our eyes?" I asked him at one point.

He burst out laughing, as if I had said something immensely funny. He wouldn't give me an answer. He fell suddenly silent, and then turned to look me in the eye again. I felt a sudden emptiness overwhelm me. His eyes were like vacuous holes. There was nothing there; no one was at home. I felt a certain horror creeping over me, a nightmarish feeling.

Then suddenly, his eyes changed and I felt I could see his very soul in his eyes.

"How do you do that?" I managed to whisper.

"You will never learn that secret, because you can't watch my eyes and watch my chest both at the same time," he said, his voice totally serious again.

"You mean you do it with your breathing?"

"I do everything with my breathing. I thought you knew that by now," he said, and with a great powerful exhale, he stood up as effortlessly as if he were weightless, and walked away.

My short week-long encounter with this man has remained a spiritual center point for my recent work in therapy research. I discovered, for instance, that the best way to encounter someone visually is to send out my personal energy and presence when I'm exhaling, and then to switch to the receiving mode when inhaling, opening myself to feeling the presence of the person I am with. In this way, visual contact becomes very quickly extremely powerful and intimate, pulsating in harmony with my breathing cycles. When I remain frozen, though, either in the receiving or broadcasting mode, intimate encounter drops away quickly.

This conscious integrating of our mode of visual expression (broadcasting and receiving) with our shifting from exhaling to inhaling appears to be one of the great conversational secrets of life. It is in essence so remarkably simple. You will find in practice, however, that it's a great challenge to remain aware of your breathing and your visual shiftings at the same time that you are talking with someone, especially if that person is not also aware of and practicing this energetic law of intimate interaction.

So please take time to experiment with this "in-out" way of breathing and seeing when you are talking with someone. It's a lifelong exploration, as are all significant spiritual disciplines. And be sure not to fixate upon the technique so much that you lose the spontaneity of your encounter experience. I recommend consciously practicing this way of conversing for just five to ten breaths at a time, and then relaxing and shifting your attention to other dimensions of the conversation. All things in moderation.

Before even employing these principles to an actual conversation, you will find it well worth your while to practice the following exercise regularly if you want to master the technique: First sit with eyes closed . . . tune into your breathing as I have taught you already . . . make no effort to breathe . . . feel the air rushing in and out your nostrils with every inhale and exhale . . . expand your awareness to include the movements in your chest and belly as you breathe . . . expand your awareness to include your whole body here in the present moment as you breathe . . . and now open your eyes, keeping your breathing as primary . . . experience sending your power and inner presence out into the world as you exhale . . . and receiving the outside world into you as you inhale.

5

Skin-to-Skin Meditations

Karen and Jim had been lovers for over a year. At first, it had been a marvelous sexual relationship, full of a special quality of tenderness and mutual understanding. But as the months progressed, they found themselves getting caught up in certain habits of sexual relating that quite honestly began to bore them. Jim especially began to find himself hungering for a new woman, to regain that sense of excitement he wanted in a relationship. Karen found herself chronically thinking while they were making love about what was going wrong, and what she could do to reawaken the passion they had known just a few months before. She wasn't willing to admit that sex always grows dull through repetition, but at the same time she was afraid it might be true.

We are going to explore in this chapter an extremely urgent and intriguing theme: how our mental habits while making love tend to lock us into shallow levels of relating, and how we can learn to break free of these chronic head-trip fixations in order suddenly to encounter our lover at deeper, nonconceptual realms of spiritual intercourse.

I happened to give a lecture on this topic at a nearby university where both Karen and Jim were grad students. She spoke with me afterward and expressed interest in doing sessions to explore her own personal mental patterns that were chronically dominating her mind. I was doing a research project at the time on a similar theme, and she became a subject/client for several months.

What she found when we began using memory as a tool for helping her to observe herself in action while making love was that even though she thought of herself as a fairly passionate, uninhibited sexual partner, in fact she was almost constantly involved in mental activity when in bed with Jim, analyzing what was going on between them, thinking about what to do next, reflecting on what had come before. Both she and Jim were intellectually very sharp, and they enjoyed their academic and philosophical relationship very much. Their problem was that they didn't know how to turn off their dominant thinking minds long enough to discover each other at deeper levels of relating.

She saw this for the first time clearly one morning during one of our early sessions. I guided her gently into a light hypnotic trance to enable her to remember her recent past in vivid detail, and soon she was reliving her sexual experience of the night before.

"We're doing our usual things, it's getting late, we've both been studying. He's taking a shower and I get out of my clothes and into bed, lighting a candle. I'm sitting there in bed naked and I'm thinking a thousand thoughts, about school, about how Jim's been relating to me, whether he wants to make love. I don't know if I want to or not, I'm tired actually. Then I feel some emotion that bothers me— a thought goes through my mind so fast I hardly see it, but it's a worry that I should be more sexy or Jim's going to leave me. That makes me start thinking about what I should do with him, and I remember making love with him last time, and how he took me so fast and it wasn't very much pleasure for me at all. I want to talk with him about how we might go about the whole thing more slowly, but I'm afraid he doesn't want to talk. Now he's coming into the room after his shower, naked. I look at him and instantly feel both a flush of bashfulness at the sight of him, because he's big already, and at the same time I feel this negative feeling. There are a dozen thoughts right under the surface of my mind, anxious, worrying thoughts. His expression is strange but I can't quite read it, like he's lost in his own world and not even quite meeting me in the eye, just looking at my breasts. He comes over and sits down beside me and right away goes for me, and when I don't respond instantly, he pulls back and just gets under the covers. Again a rush of ten thoughts at once goes through my mind, telling me to do this, do that, and before I know it, we're caught up in the same old under-the-cover sexual patterns, me doing something to stimulate him, him doing something to get me excited. We're being nice to each other, but it's like it's preprogrammed, and when he pushes into me before I'm ready, I cry out and pull back. He's so sensitive, he rolls over, and I know he's lying there thinking thoughts, maybe thinking he'd like to be with some other girl he met in class, who'd give him more what he wants in bed. And I'm lying there thinking a thousand miles an hour too, driving myself crazy. It's just terrible. I feel like there's no way out."

There is a way out, of course, but in our culture we aren't

taught what it is. From the time we're very young, we're taught that it's ideal to be thinking all the time. Our schools are radically out of balance when it comes to encouraging the full flowering of human consciousness. Everything seems to center around how clever we are, how quickly we solve intellectual problems, how deeply we can lose ourselves in cognitive thought flows.

In reality, however, as the pioneering therapist Carl Jung delineated over half a century ago and the ancient Greeks outlined several thousand years before that, there exist four equally important dimensions to human consciousness, and we become seriously imbalanced and spiritually impoverished when each of these dimensions isn't nourished properly.

The first dimension—sensation—is the vast realm of immediate perceptual inputs coming to us in the present moment through our eyes, our ears, our sense of touch, of taste, of smell. This is the dimension that lets us know we're alive on this planet in bodily form. It is also of course the crucial dimension for skin-to-skin sexual involvement.

The second dimension—emotion—is that of the ancient emotional programmings we are all born with, which include our spontaneous feelings of compassion, of fear, of anger and pain, of bliss and excitement, and all the rest. Our ability to establish heart-to-heart contact with our lover depends deeply on this level of relating.

The third dimension of human consciousness—thinking—is the one we are educated to fixate upon most, that of logical, rational thought flows as they move through our minds in conceptual patterns of symbolic meaning. This aspect of the mind enables us to share our inner feelings and understandings of life with our lover, and is certainly vital when kept in proper balance with the other three qualities of consciousness.

The fourth dimension is that mysterious realm called intuition, which refers to our direct spiritual sensing of what life is all about—an immediate realization of the deeper holistic truth related to anything upon which we might be focusing. Intuitive realms of consciousness are where we are able to expand our personal bubble of awareness to include our lover in a greater whole beyond our individual existence.

Joel Kramer in *The Passionate Mind* made the following observation about the imbalance in our culture related to these four ways of experiencing. "We have been conditioned to fixate on the thought mode. Our educational system trains us to have very active, very busy, very comparing and competitive minds. The sharper we are in our intellectual processes, the more we are rewarded by society and the world. Yet the whole nature of meditation directs itself to quieting this entire process—so that there comes into being a silence in oneself."

Karen told me she knew all this in theory. She was after all a psychology student; she had read the whole scope of literature about thought versus inner realization. However, for her, the more she thought about how to quiet her mind, the worse her befuddlement became. As Joel Kramer stated in this regard, "a mind trying to quiet itself is a very active, very busy mind. Can thought quiet itself?"

The Sensation Shift

We are almost all of us thought-flow junkies. We seem to be addicted to the stimulation and the noise and the busyness of our own thinking minds. We have been taught that we can think our way out of any problem if only we apply our logical, linear, analytic minds adequately. Employing this approach, many couples hit the relationship rocks while still fervently struggling to think their way into deeper intimacy, all the time worsening the problem through their compulsive thinking.

Perhaps the deepest quote in the Bible in this regard is the primal commandment, "Be still, and know that I am God." Whether we are dealing with sexual spirituality or any other approach to the divine in human life, there exists the absolute requirement that we first learn to be quiet, to turn off our thinking minds, if we are to know directly the presence of the Spirit in our intimate relating.

But how are we to shift away from our compulsive thinking habits, and into the deeper realms of consciousness? We have the potential to encounter the presence of the divine Spirit in our everyday sexual interactions with the body, mind, and soul of our lover. The question is, How can we break beyond our conceptual mind trips so as to make direct experiential contact with our beloved?

The answer lies as close as a copy of Carl Jung's writings: We must consciously learn to experience our lover equally through all four of the primary dimensions of human consciousness, the four vehicles that we are blessed with for encountering the world around us.

Most of us have great difficulty in shifting directly into the intuitive, spiritual mode of consciousness, especially when making love. Therefore, a more accessible dimension to begin with is the dimension of perception, of sensation, because this is usually the easiest one to awaken for people who tend to be fixated chronically on cognitive functions of the mind.

In previous chapters I have already led you a few steps into techniques for awakening the sensation dimension in sexual relating. Now we are ready to go even more intimately into this dimension as we consider how you relate with your lover in bed, with clothes off, skin-to-skin.

Hold in mind that I am not trying to eliminate the thinking part of your life experience, but to balance it with the other three. Certainly in verbal intercourse, as we have seen, there is a vast realm of sharing at conceptual levels as you struggle to gain a deeper sense of philosophical intimacy. This verbal layer of a shared life is remarkably rich and important. When there is only this one dimension, however, there exists nothing more than a point in space. The cognitive dimension must be expanded into the second dimension of sensation, then the third dimension of emotion, and finally into the fourth dimension of intuitive, spiritual union if there is to be total mystic fulfillment in a relationship.

You already know the primary act of shifting your awareness to your own breathing so that this level of sensation can be instantly awakened inside you. This is the first step Karen started doing to improve her sex life with Jim. She would practice the simple perceptual discipline of getting into bed and shifting her attention fully to her breathing, letting go of thoughts long enough to become fully aware of herself in the present moment as a breathing physical body.

"But after a few breaths," she told me after trying this a couple of times in bed, "my mind begins to go into gear again, thoughts start to take over. The habit is so strong to drift away from my body and into my mind again."

At this point, a person can either try to master serious meditative disciplines for focusing and calming the mind or do the following, which I recommend to most people in situations similar to Karen's:

Let your mind remain aware of the breathing sensations and movements, and at the same time expand your awareness to include some other region of your body where you find a pleasurable sensation already existing, such as in your feet, your fingertips, your genitals . . . if you let your mind survey your entire body, almost always you will find regions that feel good . . . and if you consciously breathe into this good feeling, it will expand . . . then often a yawn and a good whole-body stretch will take possession . . . so that there is no attention left over to shift back to thinking . . . let each new inhale expand this bubble of pleasure and satisfaction in the present moment . . . let each new exhale discharge the tensions and worries from your mind.

Karen told me a couple of weeks into our working together on this process, "I was lying in bed, breathing, relaxing, tuning into my own body, and then I turned my head and saw Jim walk into the room and something happened—I stayed in my body and didn't just lose touch with my physical self as he came over to me. It was scary, but somehow I stayed aware of my breathing, and he sat down beside me, and it seemed that he tuned into how I was feeling, too. He looked me in the eyes deeply, then looked down at my body, and I felt he really took me inside him when he looked, instead of just getting a sexual rush from my nakedness. I can't describe it except to say it was as if I'd never been with him before. I felt so exposed and vulnerable but at the same time, my body felt gigantic, powerful. Usually, it would be him reaching for me, but I was so into my body and suddenly so hungry for him, for his body, that I became the hunter for once. I had this animal power inside me, a power that was pleasure, that made me the one on top, not fighting with him because he seemed more than ready to surrender to me. I pushed him down and let him feel my full weight on top of him, and for a long moment we were both completely unmoving. I could feel myself breathing and him breathing in harmony with me, and I could feel his heart beating under me. I was completely caught up in my breathing, and after he came inside me, I stayed on top and he did something he hadn't ever done before—he let me bring myself off slowly the way I like to, the way I need to, with him getting smaller and me getting more hot down there until he finally popped out of me and I could get just the right sensation of me against him to send me into paradise. It was the first time I'd done that with a man, just completely let go and let my body find what it needed, without worrying what the man might be thinking. And the strange thing was, Jim loved it."

Nowhere to Go, Nothing to Do

Perhaps the one most important thing that couples forget to do with one another when approaching sexual intimacy is simply to take a breather and do nothing at all. We get so caught up in trying to perform properly that we busy our intimacies to death in the process.

We are also very often apprehensive about what might happen if we stopped everything and just became totally quiet for a few moments. Perhaps the excitement and sexual attraction might just fizzle out completely if we stop pushing toward orgasm. Perhaps unwanted emotions might have a chance to well up to the surface and upset our sexual encounter.

Perhaps. But if we never take a pause to find out, we never know the power and magic of complete quiet when naked and aroused with our lover. We know what it's like to come and discharge and then be quiet and at rest side by side after our passions are spent. But what if, several times during the preliminaries and even right in the middle of making love, we were to pause and tune into the stillness of intimacy?

"It was extremely scary to do that," Karen admits. "I had no idea how difficult it would be to come to a complete halt with all the kissing and touching and moving and rubbing and squeezing, all the jockeying for position and all the constant physical effort of making love. But I decided to try it. I'm getting to where I can talk more with Jim, and I said, 'Let's just be perfectly still for a moment, and see what we feel together.' I lay on my back beside him, and after at first not knowing what I was up to, he lay on his back too. God, that was an intense moment! I realized that making love has always been a frantic affair for me. As long as I'm doing something, I have control, I know what's probably going to happen next. But while we lay there side by side doing nothing, it was as if something inside my own chest suddenly expanded and there I was, in the middle of a vast world of feelings and sensations that I had never tuned into before. I could hear Jim breathing. I could feel his skin touching mine. I could feel myself breathing—and suddenly I felt my body relax. Some tension that was always inside me when making love was suddenly gone. It was delicious. Then Jim spontaneously yawned and stretched and laughed at himself, and my body did the same thing. Then there we were, side by side, doing nothing. It was such a rush! And then I felt my leg actually wanting to move up over him, not because I was thinking that was the thing to do—my leg just had the desire on its own, that's the only way I can describe it. And the sensation as my skin flowed over his, as my thigh slowly moved up and encountered his penis, that was like coming in itself. It was the most sexual thing I had ever felt—because I was relaxed and excited at the same time."

Beyond Sexual Routine:
Three Relationship Choices

Probably all of us went through the similar experience when first learning to make love of feeling extremely nervous, uncertain as to what to do—and therefore we set up habits of things to do that we found out were fairly successful in making love. We found that kissing a lot was good, and touching a lot was good, and these two actions step by step were expanded into quite a repertoire of ways to kiss and ways to touch that moved sex along to the supposedly most important goal, that of ejaculation for the male member of the team and hopefully orgasm for the female member of the duo.

In my work with marriage partners over the years, I've been constantly amazed at just how orderly and habitual the actual sexual behavior of lovers usually becomes. Routines become established so easily, and they soon act as behavioral prisons within which lovers must live with one another. We do this and then we do that and then we do this and then that, with a few variations of course, but still as a linear progression toward climax, with less and less spontaneity as time goes by.

When two people meet and are attracted to each other and begin hanging out with each other, they unfailingly bring their separate behavioral patterns from past relationships with them into the new involvement; this much is certain. As they interact with each other, they experiment with which of their old habits of lovemaking receives a positive response from the new lover, and these old patterns that work become the new patterns, intermeshed with the patterns of the other.

So a new relationship usually is not so very new, after all; it gets spiced up with some freshness from the new lover's old repertoire, and hopefully there is some spontaneous experimentation involved as well, to produce new patterns that then also become habits.

To venture into spontaneous sexual behavior with our lover is always to risk rejection, however, and since most of us fear rejection, we tend to avoid, mostly on purely unconscious levels, any truly spontaneous activity in sexual relating. Soon we find we are feeling bored with our sexual partner, and even though the reason is obvious (lack of spontaneous freedom of exploration and discovery in the relationship), we often don't realize its true cause.

Most couples reach this point, sometimes very quickly, sometimes after more time has gone by, and they are no longer highly excited by the way they relate sexually. This is a natural crisis point in a relationship, and there are four basic resolutions that couples can put into action to solve the boredom.

The first resolution is simply to live with the boredom, since there are other aspects of the relationship that are satisfying, and perhaps there are children now in the situation, and their happiness is considered primary.

The second resolution is to get sex manuals, rent porno movies, and consciously try to alter the boring sex patterns by doing new things with each other.

The third resolution is to end the relationship.

The fourth resolution is the one we are exploring in this book—that of learning to expand the deeper spiritual sense of spontaneous encounter in the relationship, so that new vistas of erotic and mystic adventure can be opened up through tapping new sexual energies.

During the sixties and seventies, it was in vogue to just dump a lover when he or she became tiring, when habits set like cement and ruined the fun of copulation. There were so many sex partners available, why waste time with an old lover when the flame had gone out?

I'm reminded of the story about Calvin Coolidge, one of our American presidents who was less than spectacular in most ways but who left us with a heritage of anecdotes that are sometimes engaging. He and his wife were visiting a model government farm one day, and they split up at some point, each going off with reporters to inspect different aspects of the farm setup. Mrs. Coolidge stopped by the chicken pens and asked the farmer beside her how often the rooster performed his sexual duties each day. "Oh, dozens of times," he responded. Obviously impressed, she replied, "Please tell that to the President."

When Mr. Coolidge made his way to the chicken pens and stood watching the rooster performing his reproductive mounting, he was told of his wife's comments.

"Same hen every time?" he asked in response.

"Oh no, sir," the farmer said. "A different one each time."

"Ah," the President said. "Please tell that to Mrs. Coolidge."

Traditionally, the males of our species have been much more likely to desire a variety of sexual partners—and to become tired with the one they have sooner—than women. Magazines such as *Playboy* took obvious delight in pointing to studies that showed how males of other mammalian species were just like men of our species. A ram, for example, will become quickly tired of sexual activity if left in the same pen with one ewe too long. But as soon as the ewe is replaced with a new female consort, the ram's sexual appetite instantly picks up, and the cycle is repeated. This phenomenon has in fact been dubbed the Coolidge Effect.

During the sexual revolution, many women tried to prove there wasn't a genetic difference between the sexes at all. Once the pill entered the picture and women no longer had to worry about becoming pregnant, it came in vogue for women to try to be just as promiscuous as men.

However, as Michael Hutchison outlined quite diligently in *The Anatomy of Sex and Power,* the sexual revolution and women's lib movements did not, in the end, result in men and women becoming exactly alike. Trying to become sexually equal to animals in other species was not necessarily a positive step forward for humankind. We possess deep emotions and bonding patterns, and these unique qualities are what make our sexual involvements so beautiful and rewarding.

The question in many women's magazines has been this: Is it really possible for two people to discover an approach to sex that transforms it into a lifelong exploration, or are all relationships fated to slip into the doldrums of sexual ennui and wither on the proverbial vine? Especially, can men be made to toe the mark, to put aside their wild animalistic sexual hunting urges so as to thrive in a monagamous relationship?

Michael Hutchison goes so far as to admit that "there's no doubt that an intelligent, imaginative, sexually creative woman can keep a man's attention, devotion, and love for a lifetime. The classic 'seven-year itch' is one that many males can become afflicted with after a single night, while some happily married males are simply not susceptible." However, he offers no insight into why some men are not susceptible. And he places upon the women the task of keeping the man's attention, devotion, and love for a lifetime, rather than seeing this challenge as mutual.

Regardless of whether individual lovers would prefer to jump from one bed to the next instead of trying to learn how to be satisfied with just one partner, the eighties brought with it a most horrible and sudden end to the sexual revolution. AIDS, in particular, and other sexually transmitted and incurable diseases such as herpes and the papilloma virus brought bed hopping to a near standstill for the majority of people. The dangers of disease came to outweigh the momentary pleasures of sexual promiscuity.

So here we are, more and more forced whether we like it or not to do the best we can with the sexual relationship we have. Certainly we can risk a bit if we so choose, and change bed partners every now and then when the passion dies. But the basic impetus in our culture now is that of finally turning concerted attention to exploring the pragmatic psychological processes through which transcendent sexual bonding comes into being and remains the vital force in a relationship, quite possibly throughout a lifetime.

While universally we mourn the victims of the diseases that have brought this change into our sexual history, at the same time we should feel blessed with the necessity of evolving into new realms of sexual fulfillment, instead of being allowed to backslide into matching our sexual performances with those of other animals, animals that, by the way, have very little orgastic pleasure in the sex act.

Most animals have much smaller brains than we do. When they copulate, they just copulate. The remarkable difference in our own copulatory experience is that we can go completely animal and yet at the same time experience with our expanded levels of consciousness the transcendent powers that come into play in the sex act. And once we make contact with this transcendent dimension in sexual relating, we actually seem to evolve into a new, advanced level of human consciousness.

An old college buddy of mine came and visited me after years apart, and we got to talking about this particular topic because both of us had by chance recently read *The Anatomy of Sex and Power*. "I was one of those guys who chased tits and ass till I was blue in the face, you must remember," he said to me. "I thought I just couldn't get enough, all through my twenties. But things changed. Women changed, too. Back in the sixties, they were as hot for a roll in the hay as a guy was, that was like paradise in some ways, back then. But I'd never go back. I got involved with several women in a row who set me straight. They were all offering me something precious, something you don't find every day, they were offering me a ticket into something deeper in making love. Each of them was a real find. But I did my usual thing and dropped them one after the other. I was afraid of them, to tell you the truth. They were wanting me to stop and sink down into some sort of closeness that made me just up and run. Three times I did that. Then something happened. I lost my drive for new virgin territory. I just got bored with the young girls. So I went back to pick up where I had left off with the women I just told you about, and every one of them had found a new man. I was the one on the outs. Three years went by that way. I finally found out what loneliness was all about, and that was good for me too. Then I met Daisy and pow, just like that, I was in love like I'd never been in love before. I never knew love could be the way it is with her. I never knew it could just get deeper and deeper all the time. But it does. Look at me, three kids, domestic as an old goat, but I feel younger than I did ten years ago. Sure I still get a rush out of the girls I run into—that's natural. But now it would be boring to run around. Daisy's got me and it's great to get got. There's this particular feeling with her, as if we're more than just a team, we're really somehow one and the same. I'm not just inside my own skin anymore, something happened and I'm not solitary anymore."

When the Bubble Pops

The problematic thing about our thinking minds is that they basically see us as being separate entities, distinct egos alone in the universe. This ability to establish a sense of distinct identity is of course essential in the development of a child into maturity. Problems arise only when we take this conceptual vision of ourselves too literally and seriously.

As documented in such popular science books as *The Tao of Physics, Biospheres*, and *The Lives of a Cell*, in reality we are not separate entities upon this planet of ours. Our physical bodies are intimately intertwined with the outside world. Our electromagnetic force field, for instance, extends out at least several feet around our physical body. The vibrations of our voice penetrate and influence everything in our immediate environment. Our actions directly intermesh with our surroundings. Our cellular life is in constant interaction with millions, even billions of tiny organisms that come and go from our body. And at the quantum-mechanics level of subatomic physics, there is really no distinct boundary between our personal bodies and the universe around us. All is one. Each particle in the universe influences every other particle, as Albert Einstein first pointed out.

What, then, is really happening when two lovers lie side by side together and quietly tune into the presence of each other? What is it that generates the feeling of suddenly being "with" your lover in the sense that you are both inside the same bubble of consciousness?

This question is as old as the hills, and yet certain scientists in the tradition of Albert Einstein are just presently giving the question a new scientific boost. According to David Bohm, for instance, one of the leading physicists in the world, the basic dynamics of quantum mechanics simply do not function unless the universe itself as an infinite whole possesses the quality of consciousness. Biologists such as Lewis Thomas of Yale University have made a strong point for the possibility that our planet as a living organism is one vast conscious being. Schools of fish and flocks of flying birds seem to have their own group consciousness. And quite possibly from a scientific as well as mystic point of view, two human beings merging through the power of love and mutual attraction are capable of expanding their individual bubbles of consciousness so that they become one greater bubble of awareness.

The basic biblical understanding of marriage stated this even more clearly in its vision of two people becoming "of one flesh" as they merge their lives together.

Whatever the scientific or religious interpretations of such merging, the inner experience is certainly powerfully valid—we do possess the ability to feel ourselves becoming more and more of one flesh with our lover/mate. Our separate consciousness possesses the ability to expand to include the consciousness of our lover within our sense of self.

Sometimes we can just sit beside our lover without any sexual charge at all and feel this sense of oneness. It is a mistake to think that there must be hot passionate energy flowing between our two bodies in order to merge in mystic harmony with our lover. Young couples sometimes blast free of their personal bubbles just by holding hands or looking in each other's eyes, as we have seen in earlier chapters.

The key point of this present chapter is that this merging seems to be inhibited when the mind is dominated by chronic thought flows. Conversely, this merging is encouraged by a silencing of the mind through focusing on perceptual levels of reality. Likewise, busyness gets in the way of mystic expansion of consciousness, while calm and quiet encourage this expansion.

I want now to encourage you to look back to your last few lovemaking sessions in this present light:

1. When you are making love these days, do you stay stuck inside your thinking mind, or can you fall silent and make direct and prolonged sensory contact with your lover?

2. Are you constantly busy and in action when making love, or do you take breathers just to lie with your lover and tune into his or her presence directly?

3. Do you hold on to your separate sense of identity during lovemaking, or can you readily let go of your sense of ego boundaries so that you can become permeated by the presence of your lover?

Give yourself plenty of time to pause, put the book away after reading this paragraph . . . relax . . . tune into your breathing . . . begin to remember your last lovemaking experience . . . and reflect upon the three questions I just raised as you relive your sexual encounter.

The Ultimate Appetite

In certain ways, sexual intercourse is no different from a good meal—it is satisfying a certain hunger that arises naturally in the human body by providing what is needed to satiate that appetite. Hunger is a built-in mechanism to make sure we get what we need to survive, even if our higher cognitive levels of functioning forget we have these basic needs. Thus we can be lost in work or play, completely oblivious to our body for hours on end—and suddenly feel the growing sense of hunger inside us, pushing to get our attention.

Hunger is an experience in which we feel a pressure inside us, perform certain step-by-step procedures that satisfy the pressure, and then for a period of time have no hunger of that type at all. Then quite predictably the hunger comes again, and we do the same basic procedures in order to relieve it.

At this basic level of biological functioning, the hunger for sex is a very goal-oriented phenomenon. We have an itch to be scratched. We have a genital pressure to relieve. The goal is in the future, and everything we do is a push toward that future sense of release and satisfaction. The present moment isn't the key focus of consciousness until we reach the actual point of orgasm or ejaculation and then for just a short moment find ourselves in the bliss of the here and now, only to drop out of it as soon as the sensation of release has passed.

It is this level of sexual interaction that the thinking mind tunes in to best, since, as we have seen already, thinking is a past-future process of the mind itself. As soon as the thinking mind feels the proverbial itch, it begins to remember past sexual experiences where orgasm was attained and hunger abated. From this storehouse of past experiences, the mind then anticipates a future experience of similar effect and begins to motivate the body to behave in ways that will lead to the desired result. Once the release is attained, the mind then shifts to other hungers that might arise. Another past-future fixation is established in the mind to consume one's power of attention.

When the hunger becomes acute, then it shifts into what we call a craving, in which we become quite compulsively panting after satisfaction of our hunger. Nothing else is important to us except release from our craving.

This once again is the basic way in which all other animals function, both in terms of hungering for food and hungering for sexual intercourse. We have this programming in our genes in order to keep us alive and procreating regardless of extenuating circumstances. Many people, as I'm sure you've noticed, tend to remain at this level of functioning throughout their lives.

As human beings, however, we are lucky enough to possess the remarkable potential for transcending these basic animal hunger/satiation patterns, not through eliminating them but through transforming them into higher levels of conscious behavior. In essence, we learn to use the intense energetic charge that instinctive hungers generate in our bodies to empower expanded levels of present-moment awareness. This at heart is the biological nature of spiritual unfolding.

From this understanding, you can see why in this book we are exploring ways to shift from past-future goal-oriented mind states in sexual relating to present-moment non-goal mind states. We are learning how to use sexual energies to blast us into spiritual orbit, so that we can prolong the ecstatic experience that comes with sexual arousal and focus our attention at the direct center of the source of our hunger.

"It's like this for me," a male friend explained. "When I was younger, I was totally caught up in coming. Masturbation was something to do as quickly as I could, because what I really craved was the feeling of coming. The buildup was just something to get finished with as soon as I could. When I started having intercourse for real, I was still caught up in this masturbation routine, panting for the big blow and not much bothering with the preliminaries. It took me a long time, I hate to admit, before I started to learn how to savor the preliminaries, to sit on the charge, so to speak. Now finally, I've gotten to where I like to postpone coming for as long as I can. I want to stay right in the middle of the magic for as long as possible. Once I come, that's it. Before I come, it's gotten to where I'm in pure bliss, pure ecstasy. What took me so long was getting to where I could handle the intensity, getting to where I could relax and feel at home right in the middle of the intensity. What I'm trying to say is that I can get right to the point of coming and then stay at that point, sometimes back away from it, then get up to it again, and stretch things out for a long time. It's having your cake and eating it too. And it's pretty much something that takes time to master. I'm just starting to get the hang of it myself."

From Hunger to Desire

I find the word *desire* very apt for describing the higher levels of sexual passion that lie beyond our basic biological programming for sexual interaction. Desire certainly has its roots in our biological hungering for sexual release. But with desire, new dimensions are added to the basic mix of genital passions, especially the crucial dimension of love, of hungering not only for genital release but for heart contact and shared emotional intimacies.

Our desire for someone is not based in the compulsion to attain genital orgasm or ejaculate. Desire is experienced as a longing for skin contact, for penetration of the emotional membrane that separates us from our lover. Desire is ultimately the passion to lose our sense of isolated ego identity and to be blown upon the wings of sexual abandon into infinite spiritual realms of being.

Sexual intercourse is, of course, often defined by the act of physical penetration. In very real terms of experience, there is also such a thing as spiritual penetration. Curiously though, this penetration is not a male-female dynamic. It is something that happens simultaneously in both directions, at the moment when both lovers open their hearts, open their spiritual selves to the other. Suddenly, pop! Two bubbles become one. Ego membranes have become permeable. Boundaries are gone, at least for a short time.

It is this level of spiritual penetration and sexual intensity that is sustained by postponing the orgasm experience and indulging in the present-moment of preorgasm intimacy. This is where the real art of lovemaking comes into play—not in terms of masterful technique or overpowering seduction but instead in terms of simply relaxing into the energetic force field that comes into being when two sexually aroused people hold their attention upon each other and upon their own internal center at the same time.

Considerable maturity is required to blow up the transpersonal sexual bubble and yet keep it intact. It is a magical balancing act that certainly never gets old, because each time we do it, many variables are changed from before. We must rely not on past experience but on the present moment, just as a tightrope walker must.

There are two directions we can fall when the bubble pops. We can either fall into orgasm, which ends the love-making's intensity for at least a while, or we can fall into a temporary state of prepassion, in which sexual desire becomes suddenly less. Either direction is acceptable of course. But as we will see in chapter seven, dropping back momentarily from the edge of climax several times during lovemaking is truly a masterful approach to gaining increased depth and energetic distance from a sexual encounter.

What are your patterns in this regard? Be honest with yourself, look to your recent lovemaking bouts, and see whether you push quickly to climax or whether you and your lover enjoy delaying gratification in order to relish the fine charge of energy you are participating in together.

The Bottomless Relationship

At a certain point, couples either discover the infinite magic of focusing on preclimax pleasures and spiritual energies or they burn out on the sexual relationship; at least this has been my long-term observation. Acting out the animal hunger for sex is such a limited experience for a human being in itself that, of course, one must change sexual partners often in order to keep interested. Only when the discovery of the preclimax present moment is made can there be a healthy lifetime to the relationship.

The trick of all spiritual techniques working with sexual energies is to shift the sexual charge quickly away from just the genital region of the body. First this vital creative energy is encouraged to come rushing up into the heart region, so that the passion is transformed into compassion. Then the transformed energy is sent farther up into the higher spiritual centers at the top of the head. As I mentioned earlier, there are seven major energy centers in the human nervous system, and true spiritual awakening through sexual love happens when all seven of the energy centers are equally charged. This is the key process of traditional nonintercourse Kundalini meditation, as well, which I have described at length in *Kundalini Awakening*.

As the sexual energy rises up through the body, there is another amazing dimension to this energy-flow experience while making love, which all mature couples also come to know intimately and to surrender to more and more fully. Not only is primal energy experienced as rising up through the body as if from the procreative bowels of the earth, enflaming and empowering the genitals and then heart and soul. Energy also can be felt at a certain crucial point while making love as flowing down into the body from above— but only after the genital energy has been guided up into the heart!

This dynamic is described in almost every ancient spiritual tradition in the world where sexual realization is merged with spiritual realization. Sexual partners sometimes tap almost instantly into this total energetic experience during their first sexual encounters, only to lose the quality of merging later on. Many couples never manage to let go of the goal-oriented fixation long enough to make the discovery. Many couples sometimes manage to blunder into the bliss of whole-body awakening and final orgasm now and then without knowing quite what they are doing or how to encourage the experience. And, of course, some couples learn how consciously to dance the sexual dance together in such a way as to create regularly a spiritual experience right in the center of their sexual experience.

One thing is clear. The deeper dimensions of spiritual

union during sexual intercourse are best discovered by staying with the same partner over a long duration. This is true
simply because there is such a vast realm to explore, and one
must know one's partner very well in order to continue
expanding into new realms. The level of mutual trust determines the level of expansion. And the level of expansion
underlies our ability to totally surrender our separate identities to the present moment.

In this present moment of relating, as Ken Keyes has
stated in his *Handbook to Higher Consciousess,* "you begin to
enjoy every second as a fulfilling whole in itself. Whatever
happens as the flow of love unfolds is enough. Your mind
is not concerned with what will be happening a few seconds
or a few minutes from now. Hence, it is not grasping. It is
not manipulating. It is not striving. It is just flowing completely with your feelings and the feelings of your partner—
and the nowness of the environment around you."

When True Union Happens

There exists yet another level of consciousness that can be
attained while making love. I will speak in depth of this in
the final chapters, but let me mention it just briefly in this
context as well.

In the realms of the heart, desire mixes with hunger and
we have compassion, the basic power of love. Sometimes,
at a certain point in sexual intercourse, like a gift from God,
even desire itself seems to pass away, and a pure state of
being beyond desire is attained for a short time. This is the
ultimate state of meditation of any kind. When it suddenly
comes over a couple entwined in sexual love, it is certainly

the most remarkable experience possible to mortal beings—because suddenly the transpersonal bubble of consciousness that unites two people expands infinitely in all directions, releasing all sense of pressure or time. The sexually united couple merges with the infinite godhead as the infinite consciousness of the universe itself is experienced momentarily by the couple.

"I can't speak of what happened quite," a friend confided in me a few days after this experience happened to her and her husband. "I was already feeling very deeply one with him for perhaps ten minutes. We were sitting in the yab-yum position; that's the only position that enables us to stay still for longer periods. And then suddenly I was simply gone, he was gone. I felt the bottom drop out from under me and at the same time I felt that, well, that I was God, not just one with God, but . . . you see, words can't describe it, there is nothing to compare with what happened. But it happened. All I can say is that the word *love* comes closest to what we experienced, infinite love, down here in the heart but also just everywhere. I might have stayed in that state forever except that—and here I get red in the face from the memory—he suddenly started to move, started to come, and he blasted like a volcano, the energy was so great inside him."

This is perhaps the ultimate experience that can come in a sexual relationship. And to attain this spiritual bliss and mystic realization in a sexual involvement, it is actually necessary only to explore consciously over a period of time the basic principles I have already outlined:

1. Both before and while sharing in sexual intercourse, maintain your awareness of your breathing as the most central and important focus of your moment-to-moment attention.

2. Let your exhales feel equal to your inhales so that you don't so overcharge yourself that you have to come quickly.
3. Regularly pause and relax even in the midst of sexual passion so that you can regain your deeper center and expand your bubble of awareness to include your partner.
4. Instead of fixating your attention on genital stimulation, regularly shift your attention up to your heart region so that there can come a flow of creative sexual energy up into your higher energetic centers.
5. Consciously remember to open yourself to the mystic experience of light and energy flowing down from above through your head, heart, and into your genitals and feet so that you become balanced with earthly and spiritual energies.
6. To the best of your ability, be equally conscious at all times of yourself and your sexual partner.
7. Rather than holding your breathing tightly in anticipation of genital pleasures and release, relax your breathing into spiritual expansion.

In the days and weeks and literally years to come, you can put these basic guidelines into action in your love life, and expand your preorgasm experience into regular contact with the divine within and beyond you and your lover.

6

Ecstasy
Beyond Fantasy

Ursula was very much in love with Joshua; they were already making plans to get married in a few months. But she was plagued by a dimension of their lovemaking that seemed wrong to her but that refused to go away. At a certain point during intercourse, she would find herself drifting into sexual-fantasy land instead of being completely in the present moment with Joshua. The fantasies were the same kind she used to indulge in as a teenager when she first learned to give herself sexual pleasure—pretending to have sex with ideal lovers, mythic he-men. She had talked with Joshua about her fantasies, and to her surprise he had found it exciting that she indulged in them. He told her he did the same thing, that sex was all about fantasizing while making love. But she still felt in her heart that all this fantasizing while having intercourse was keeping her and Joshua from really encountering each other at lev-

els she was hungering for more and more. Her problem
was that she didn't know how to break free of the
habit, it was so strongly ingrained in her.

This chapter is very likely to cause considerable controversy
because it runs directly against the grain of popular sex talk
these days. Such best-selling books as *For Each Other* by
Lonnie Barbach, *Being a Woman* by Toni Grant, and *Sexual
Secrets* by Nik Douglas and Penny Slinger, for instance,
consider erotic fantasy to be an important and often essential
element in lovemaking.

Certainly up to a point, erotic fantasy plays a natural part
in a human being's overall sexual repertoire. It is also quite
true that people suffering from serious sexual inhibitions
can benefit from employing erotic fantasy to awaken passion
both before and while making love. The point I am making
in this book is that at a certain point, in order to attain a
higher level of spiritual intimacy in sexual relationships, fantasy simply must be put away completely, just as drugs must
be put aside, conversations silenced, and chronic thought
flows quieted.

Ursula tells from personal experience how fantasies were
interfering with the levels of sexual merging she desired.
"When I began falling in love with Joshua, there was certainly a lot of daydreaming and fantasy going on," she told
me. "That's how it's always been with lovers in my life. I
guess it's because in between relationships, I spend nights
alone and keep my spirits up by making myself feel good.
Masturbation is almost completely fantasy for me, I hardly
have even to touch myself at all in order to get excited.
But then when I meet someone in the real world who
excites me, my erotic daydreams continue to come into my
mind, especially when we get down to clothes-off relating.
I'll be half in the present moment, feeling my boyfriend's

body and touch and penetration and everything, and half off in my safe fantasy world, imagining my ideal lover on top of me, inside me. These old fantasies, with new variations, of course, rush into my mind every time I make love. I guess you could say I'm addicted to them. Even when I have a real live man in my arms like Joshua, whom I love very much, I more and more drift away into my inner fantasy worlds as the intensity of the lovemaking grows. And when I finally come, I'm just gone. The man I was with before Joshua complained about how he felt me going away when we made love. I think he left me partly because of that. Now I've found a man who does the same thing I do, goes away, too—but this time I'm the one who doesn't like it."

Ursula had reached a critical and very exciting point in her love life. She had become conscious of her chronic mental patterns while making love, and was ready to break free of them. This realization of the need to move beyond fantasy is a point of deep maturity in one's sexual being.

Regardless of where you are in this natural progression toward more awareness of your mental habits, you should find this following discussion helpful. We are going to look closely at how the human mind actually functions when we fantasize. We're also going to explore how we initially set up our personal techniques for stimulating ourselves sexually with erotic fantasies, so that we can see clearly how to transcend fantasy activities in our minds when we want to be totally in the experiential present moment with our lover. This is a beautiful theme, since both indulging in erotic fantasy and the transcending of erotic fantasy are extremely satisfying experiences.

Intense Excitement in Early Life

In *Magical Child*, Joseph Chilton Pearce has shown how fantasy begins very early in a child's life, congruently with the ability to talk, around the age of two or so. I've been watching this with my second son, who is two and a half right now, and whose fantasy capacity is already quite remarkable. For instance, he's flown in an airplane only four times in his life, and not at all in over a year, and yet just this morning we were sitting side by side in a low easy chair in the living room, and he was holding his two hands up and imagining flying an airplane through the sky. The pleasure he felt while acting out this fantasy was perhaps not as intense as specifically sexual pleasure will be later on in his life, but he was definitely quite ecstatically transported for minutes on end.

This ability to fantasize isn't something we are taught how to do; it's quite a natural spontaneous occurrence in the human psyche, a mental phenomenon that underlies the entire superstructure of consciousness itself. Our basic ability to think about anything at all requires that we be able to remember past experiences, and then project them into future possibilities. This transformation of memory images from the past into present-moment imaginings is most definitely what fantasy is all about. And there would be no problem-solving power to the human mind at all if we didn't have this ingrained genetic capacity for fantasizing. Our survival depends on it.

Before puberty occurs, our capacity for ecstatic experiencing is already quite magnificent. What seems to happen at puberty is that the nervous system's whole-body potential for excitement fixates in the region of the genitals rather than being dissipated throughout the body. Before this, instead of specifically genital charging and discharging, a more diffuse charging and discharging happens during excitement. Still, the ecstatic experience of a preteen can be just as high as the sexual charge of a mature person. One has only to watch children at play to see just how high and euphoric they can become, given even half a chance. I happen to live just across the way from the grammar school in my community, and when recess begins, the sounds that come from the playground are full of ecstatic shouts and screams and laughter—a truly pre-erotic cacophony of human beings in extreme states of pleasure!

You were almost certainly a child who got intensely excited from time to time. Let me give you a moment or two to pause in your reading so you can look back and remember just how your body felt when you became excited. Was this feeling in any way similar to sexual excitement?

Prepubescent Sexual Feelings

Even at an early age, a child is capable of quite intense sexual feelings. It is a great mistake to assume that children have no sexual sensations or fantasies before puberty. Toddler boys most definitely get erections and are extremely sensitive genitally, and little girls in a relatively free environment will take great pleasure in innocently stroking their clitoris.

The great sexual transformation that comes with puberty is not, therefore, a total alteration in the pleasure patterns of children but rather the special development of the capacity to attain genital orgasm, to get pregnant, to ejaculate, to build a sexual charge and release it through genital channels.

Long before such genital action comes alive, young children have already developed much of the groundwork for their erotic fantasy life by observing adults in their everyday environment in the process of sexual charging and acting out patterns that lead to discharge. Little kids are remarkably knowledgeable sexually by the time they're six or seven years old. They've seen Mommy kissing Daddy and who knows whom else; they've seen people getting all hot and bothered sexually in their presence. Most kids have even sneaked moments of forbidden observation of intense sexual foreplay and often full intercourse as well. The sexual attitudes and behaviors of adults in a child's environment will strongly determine the types of fantasies children develop.

Some parents openly express their sexual feelings and behaviors in the presence of their children. Other parents hide from their children their feelings and activities related to sexual arousal and discharge. Studies have shown that parents who hide their sexual activities and feel secretive, guilty, and ashamed of their sexuality raise children who tend to be full of fantasies about forbidden sexual behavior. These children of inhibited parents tend to become adults who masturbate excessively, crave access to pornographic material, and, from my therapy observations, remain caught most chronically in fantasy activity while making love.

What do you remember of your own childhood experiences? Did you get to see early in life what natural uninhibited human sexual relating is all about, or did you have to try secretly to put together bits and pieces of the sexual puzzle, and generate a somewhat distorted fantasy image of what romantic sexual relating must be like?

Take some time to delve into your memory banks again, and relive the intense times in your childhood when you saw forbidden things, when you discovered what adults do, when you were excited by the sexual activities, either covert or up-front, of sexually aroused teenagers and adults in your childhood environment.

Pubescent Daydreams

For most of us, almost our entire sexual experience during puberty was of the fantasy kind. Very few of us received any sexual initiation or education of the hands-on type. Our parents and community strictly forbade any overt sexual activity. In most regions, a sixteen-year-old boy getting caught having intercourse with a fifteen-year-old girl can even be sent to jail as a sex offender. And for a girl honestly to express her desire for sexual contact, and to seek out this contact, is to risk a terrible condemnation by church and state, school authorities, and most peers. Quite bluntly, we are a society deathly afraid of the natural sexual energies we are all born with and wish to express during puberty. Michael Hutchison hits the nail on the head in *The Anatomy of Sex and Power* when he says, "America is obsessed with sex. There's no doubt—American life is drenched in sexuality. Our lives, our thoughts, are more intensely sexual than ever before. But that doesn't mean we like it. The result is a unique cultural schizophrenia that causes us to spend most of our time in a state of sexual arousal while pretending to disapprove of the very thing that's arousing us."

Children brought up in our culture are chronically saturated with sexual images and provocations. Television panders to our craving for soft-porn stimulation. Schools are plagued with kids who are imitating their TV role models, trying to be sexy adults at the age of ten or even younger, and already addicted to the pervading sense of sexual fixation and often downright perversion in which their parents are caught up.

When I was a ten- to twelve-year-old kid, only thirty-some years ago, most of my sexual fantasies were from real-life sources, since the media wasn't so dominant back then, at least in my particular environment. Progressively, however, children's fantasies have been more and more fueled by sexual ideals and mores presented on television. This shifting from real-life models to flat two-dimensional television models for sexual behavior and fantasy has had a drastic effect on the fantasy life of new generations. The result, as psychological studies document, has been a flattening of the imaginative function of the human mind over the last quarter of a century. Who knows what the final result of this reduction of imagination to a common and quite commonplace norm will be? Certainly within the scope of sexual fantasy, a lowered level of sexual fantasy can be expected to lead to a lowered level of pleasure among sexual couples.

Our saving grace in this situation, however, is that there does exist a realm of consciousness beyond conditioned programming and fantasy activity, and certainly beyond the confines of television mentality. This is the realm, as we have seen, of mystic awakening into the sexual potency of the eternal present moment. Much of my aim in writing this book is to offer a way out of the chronic mind states that we have been forced into by the mechanized, commercialized, dehydrated condition of our cultural environment. There is absolutely no need to remain victimized by our childhood and the ongoing adult brainwashing we receive through television exposure.

Curiously, even pubescent children often find themselves quite spontaneously transcending the dullness of their cultural fantasy programming, even before they begin making love and encountering the transformational power of the orgasm experience. Often in my therapy work, through the power of light hypnotic trance and age-regression techniques, I have led clients back to relive their actual fantasy experiences during puberty, and I've been awed by the explosive mythic content of these experiences. I have yet, in fact, to work with a client or subject in this regard without the person being able to remember at least one transcendent experience during puberty of total, expansive spiritual communion related to sexual excitement.

The human organism is truly a remarkable phenomenon. Our minds are so easily programmed on certain levels, but our spirits remain intact despite whatever conditioning we have received. I worked quite a bit in East Berlin about eight years ago, surreptitiously crossing the border on day passes every couple of weeks to meet with a group of psychiatrists there who had read a couple of my books (which were banned in East Germany and had to be smuggled in) and wanted to learn more deeply about certain of my consciousness-expansion programs. Here were adults who had been seriously brainwashed from birth in most cases to believe that there is no transcendent spiritual dimension to life. And yet they were secretly quite in tune with their mystic dimensions of consciousness, struggling to keep their spiritual flames alive in the midst of the depressing conditionings being laid on their heads daily in the Communist system.

"I was very much caught up in the Communist programming at school until I entered into puberty," one East Berlin woman told me. "Then everything seemed to explode inside me. I felt a wild passion that blew me free of what they had taught me to believe. I suddenly saw through my teachers.

I felt free. The sexual energy saved me. This remains one of my main lessons in life, that the sexual energy is our natural gateway into freedom."

The Mystic Bubble Expands

As I mentioned earlier, human beings seem to come awake to their own spiritual presence right as they first learn to fly upon the wings of overt sexual energies in puberty. Roughly from the ages of five to ten, our minds are busy forming concepts to represent our sense of separateness from the outside world, from our parents, from nature. We create the essential bubble of self-identity that sustains us throughout life.

However, then without expecting it or asking for it, along comes a sudden transformation inside our bodies and minds that sometimes expands our bubble momentarily so that we realize there is more to us than just our own bodies and our personal concepts of who we are. Suddenly we encounter the infinite beyond, the mystic depths, the sexually charged realms of ecstatic union with a greater reality.

Rudy Rucker, one of our great scientific writers and scholars, has expressed this happening in *Infinity and the Mind* by coining the new term *interface enlightenment*, referring to the capacity of human consciousness to interface with the spiritual presence that surrounds personal consciousness—what is beginning to be called "transpersonal consciousness," and, in extension, "planetary consciousness."

A client of mine recently expressed this transformational pubescent experience in the following words. "I was lying in bed one night when I was, oh, eleven or so, caught up in my new habit of imagining sexual things about girls I knew in school. For some reason, the fantasies that night affected me more intensely than before. I guess new sex hormones were getting released into my system and my whole body was rushing for the first time with that wild sexual energy. Anyway, right in the middle of rubbing my penis under the covers and dreaming of touching this girl's breasts, I felt a rocket blasting off up my spine, and without hardly realizing what was happening, I was squirting stuff out my penis—and right at that moment I experienced white light, pure spiritual bliss for moments on end. Only now when I look back and remember what I actually felt do I see that the experience that sometimes comes to me these days in deep meditation is the same experience that came to me just from masturbating that first time."

This is where childhood fantasy leads us—to encountering the divine spiritual potency of life for the first time in our personal lives. Suddenly, the fantasies in our minds activate sexual energies that momentarily blow away our bubble of personal reality as we expand infinitely into the white light of sexual and mystic realization.

Thus we discover in puberty, or at some point later on when we consciously enter into the orgasm experience, that there is a way out, a way beyond our own conditioned selves. "Now I see why I have this desire for something more than I have with Joshua," Ursula said after I had led her back into remembering her first flashes of release when she was thirteen. She hadn't reached an orgasm then. Instead, as happens often with girls, she had had a sudden explosion of sexual energies through her entire nervous system. "I had forgotten completely about that experience until just now," she said. "How is it that we forget something so intense?"

In fact, most people forget the majority of their early

sexual encounters with the divine. It is often a frightening experience for young people to have their ego boundaries blown out from under their conceptual feet, and to discover that where they thought there was something solid, there is instead an infinite realm of mystic consciousness. It is natural to be afraid of this infinite beyond, especially in our present culture, where children receive very little honest training and preparation for such an encounter—in fact, where most adults fail to admit to the reality in their own lives.

However, as adults, we still desire renewed contact with the depths of our soul that we came into contact with as teenagers, through sexual awakening. We know deep down that there exist vast realms of intimate encounter at the heart of the sexual experience.

Let me give you another breather from this flow of words we are engaged in, so that you can put the book aside after reading this paragraph and look back into your own pubescent experiences to where your budding sexual fantasies awakened explosive mystic energies and visions in your mind. (I encourage you to exercise regularly this ability to relive your past in more and more intense vividness. Practice makes perfect in this regard. And to tap into your early sexual/spiritual experiences is instantly to reawaken the innocent power and clarity of your earlier self.) See what memories spring effortlessly, spontaneously to mind as you relax for a few minutes . . . close your eyes if you want to at some point . . . tune into your breathing experience as your constant friend and anchor in the present moment . . . and turn your power of attention back to your early sexual experiences in puberty, as you found your nervous system suddenly enflamed by a biochemical rush of hormones that woke your mind and body up to a new level of consciousness and communion with the divine within you and around you.

Your Favorite Sexual Daydreams

Human beings have a vast variety of fantasies when it comes to things that turn them on sexually. Many adults, for instance, remain fixated on early childhood experiences that pushed them into extreme states of excitement, such as beatings by their father or mother, passionate horse rides, dangerous encounters of one kind or another, or fascinations with hosiery and other artifacts of sexual intercourse.

The reason we daydream, of course, is because it stimulates good feelings inside us. We discover that once we have a pleasurable or exciting experience in real life, we can continue to milk this experience for further stimulation and pleasure by remembering the experience. And almost always, our fantasy minds begin to play with these actual memories, mixing them with other similar memories, letting them grow within our minds in unique configurations of fantasy.

It is a psychological cliché that human beings seek out pleasure in their lives. This is a genetic programming of extreme importance, certainly in sexual relating but also in all aspects of daily routine. We run our entire lives based on habits that help us to avoid obnoxious and traumatizing feelings, and that at least somewhat predictably enable us to have stimulating and pleasureful feelings.

The magic of fantasy is that even if our real lives are a bore or downright repressive, we can turn to the fantasies inside our own minds and make ourselves feel good, even stimulate potent charges of sexual pleasure inside us that we can then release through masturbation or intercourse. In this way, fantasy is our best friend—it is a dimension of life that we have under our own control, and, as recent sexual-liberation movements have lauded, it enables us to feel at least somewhat free of less dependent on other people for our own well-being and sense of pleasure in life.

However, unless a person is seriously neurotic and afraid of real-life encounters, he or she tends to prefer the real thing when it is available, compared with the fantasy experience of the real thing. In the same way that eating a good meal is ultimately more satisfying than imagining eating that meal, having sexual intercourse with an actual human being is more satisfying to us than *imagining* making love with that person.

If sex was nothing more than what many of our experts of the last few decades tried to convince us of, then masturbation and fantasy would be quite as good as actual human encounter for sexual release and fulfillment. If all we are after in sex is to blow off our energetic charges, then masturbation is great and quite less complicated than human interaction.

In fact, however, sex, as we are seeing in these pages and as you know yourself, is vastly more than genital release. It is an encounter that transforms us, that moves us beyond our own minds and brings us into communion with the reality beyond the confines of our egos.

Once fantasy is put in its place and ceases to dominate our lives, then it can be enjoyed quite pleasurably, and put aside at the proper time.

First of all, let's explore your own favorite times and places for sexual daydreaming, and the contents of your erotic fantasies. Then we will end the chapter by exploring techniques for consciously learning to move beyond these fantasies when you so desire.

Where and when do you, tend to slip into sexual daydreams to give yourself a rush of pleasure? Do you do this while going home from work in the car or in the bus or subway? Do you fantasize as you drift off to sleep? Do you sneak off to bed and fantasize to stimulate masturbatory experiences? Do you catch yourself fantasizing right in the middle of lovemaking? Look back over the last few days and see where and when you have indulged in interior sexual dreams.

Old Flames That Keep Burning

Most people have had sexual encounters in their past that were quite delicious, and that they enjoy running through their minds to stimulate themselves sexually. Often while making love, a person will find old lovers popping into mind, like ghosts who haven't quite given up the ship.

This is an extremely important question to explore. How are we to relate with beautiful erotic experiences we have had in the past, with lovers we have once felt deeply in tune with on many levels of intimacy? Are we to try to obliterate them from our minds and fantasies so that we feel completely loyal to our new love? Or are we to cherish their memory and keep them alive in our fantasies?

"For a long time, I felt possessed by Judy," a man I know told me one evening. "You remember how much I loved her. I thought she was finally the one and only for me, and then suddenly she was gone. I'd never been so in love, I'd never had that kind of sex with a woman. And I'd never had my heart broken quite that hard. Usually, I'd been the one causing the heartbreak. So after she was gone, I'd lie around imagining her still with me. I could have remarkable solitary times doing that. Then I met Angie and fell in love again, but Judy was still there. Right in the middle of intercourse, I'd find myself imagining that Angie was Judy. I never told

Angie about this though until recently, when it all changed. I tried to wipe Judy out of my memory, but she kept coming back right when I'd surrender to that overwhelming feeling just before I'd come. Finally, I had to jump on a plane and go clear across the country and see her face-to-face again. That did the trick somehow. Now I think of her a lot, and feel good about the times we had. But she's in the past and I can stay with Angie right up to the end and afterward, too."

What about you, do you have an old lover or two who populate your mind, and if so, how do you handle this? Do you feel guilty about sometimes overlaying this old lover, this old flame, upon your present-moment sexual partner? Do you still have solitary times when you lie in bed and remember the old sexual experiences with someone in your past?

Pause and remember the dominant people from your erotic past who still come into your mind . . . explore how, in fact, you feel about their presence in your new love affair if you are now in one.

The Idyllic Scene of Conquest

People often also have fantasies not about a particular person from their past but about a particular situation or setting where they feel their sexuality coming most alive. Some people daydream of being back in an idyllic setting in ancient Greece or some other romantic place in their imagination. They imagine certain sequences of action in which passions are awakened step by step. Usually, these sequences and situations are ones that were established during early pubes-

ECSTASY BEYOND FANTASY**145**

cent fantasy trips when an ideal romantic notion was strong in the heart. The fantasy pattern remains long into adulthood because it evokes such pure powerful erotic feelings in the person's sexual body each time it is reawakened.

"I guess I'm one of those women who's addicted to romance books and who yearns for the ideal dreams to come true," a client told me. "I prefer historical romances mostly, but they have to be quite sexy, and where they aren't, my mind makes up the difference. I get so excited I can hardly breathe sometimes, just like I used to when I was in school. God, I love it! Imagining some mystic man touching me, ripping off my dress, violating me. My husband never assaults me, and I suppose I'd be scared to death if he did. I've never acted out my fantasies, I don't think I want to. I just love the passion I feel when I read those books, and after I've read one, I just have to bring myself off, it's completely different from making love. Sometimes I think I'm taking passion away from my sex life with my husband, this is true, but you see, I'm a junkie. I can't stop myself, it's a habit I've had since I was twelve. How do you break that kind of habit? I've just got to have intensity in my life, and real life is just downright dull."

This woman came to me because she knew she had a problem, that she wasn't getting out of life what she really hungered for sexually. Her case is such a common one these days. Romance books dominate the market in the publishing world. The stark statistic is that fully 40 percent of all book sales are of the soft-porn romance genre. Tens of millions of women are seriously addicted to this form of fantasy stimulation.

In and of itself, as we have seen, such stimulation through fantasy is great. We have the right to feel intensely at sexual levels. Masturbation, erotic self-stimulation, is perfectly natural and psychologically healthy to a degree. Only when fantasy becomes an addiction, when it takes away from real-life possibilities, should it be considered a problem. But by this definition, millions of women do have this problem, and certainly let me say in the same breath that men do the same basic thing, getting their new *Penthouse*s or other erotic publications and breathlessly opening the virgin pages to see what new visual images are being offered to stimulate a fantasy sexual encounter with an ideal female consort.

I personally disagree with such leaders as Richard Nixon on down to our present gallant President in their claims that sexually explicit material should be forcefully eliminated from the public eye. Getting rid of pornography does not get rid of the desire for pornography. We must evolve into a sexually more healthy nation in general, not try just to outlaw expressions of our sexual repression. Recent studies have shown that sex offenders, for instance, look at less pornography than does the average American. Pornography doesn't lead to sexual violence; it simply keeps people locked up in fantasy land instead of breaking the addiction so that they can have deeper transpersonal sexual experiences.

The problem with masturbation spiritually is quite simple. In masturbation, there is no expanding of one's consciousness to include another actual human being in one's bubble of awareness. In self-stimulation, the magic of transpersonal awakening is not possible. The whole experience happens inside one's mind, rather than expanding to take in deeper levels of reality. We get a rush, but we don't gain transformation. And the more we become addicted to the biochemical injection of sex-arousal chemicals into our system through fantasy and masturbation, the harder it is to break free of this and venture out into the real and sometimes emotionally dangerous world in order to risk higher levels of sexual encounter.

Take a look at your own habits in this regard, not to judge yourself but to gain that potent stimulus of insight and growth through seeing clearly your own habits in action. Do you expend a lot of your sexual energies in fantasy activity, and if so, what are your usual fantasies?

Breaking the Erotic-Fantasy Habit

As we have seen, the aim in dealing with our fantasy habits is not to judge them all as negative and try to get rid of them completely. Fantasy is one of the true treasures of consciousness when kept in proper balance and not allowed to take over too much of our awareness.

But what can be done when fantasy seems to have taken over the ship of consciousness? There are several pragmatic steps to follow in transcending the habit of chronic fantasy activity when it actually becomes a distraction in sexual relating. These steps are variations on the basic attention-shifting techniques you have already begun to learn. I'll outline the steps in a moment so that you have a clear vision of them.

The key thing to hold in mind about habits is that we can never actually obliterate a habit from our minds. It remains a potential response to provoking situations throughout our lives. What we can do is either decondition a self-defeating habit through punishment and push it down a few notches in our response repertory or, much better, consciously develop a new habit that gives us more satisfaction, so that we naturally choose the new over the old when we do choose.

If we choose the second solution, which is usually the best approach in fantasy reduction, then the first thing to hold in mind as a cognitive stimulus to action is this: We are limited beings in terms of such things as sexual energy, because our biochemical functioning is a limited bodily process. If we release too much of our sexual energies in fantasy activity and masturbatory routines, we simply won't have enough vital energy left for the more spiritual and direct heart-to-heart encounters in sexual relating. To see this trade-off clearly is to make the first step in breaking beyond chronic fantasy activity. Along with this step, there are several others that, when mastered while making love, provide effortless and pleasurable passage beyond fantasy fixations. You have been practicing variations on these themes for transcending other habits in your intimate involvements. Let me outline these steps clearly in this new context so that you have them firmly in mind, and then you can, over the next weeks and months at your own leisure, apply them to your sexual encounters until you have established them as a new sexual habit of mind and body when making love.

Observe Your Fantasy Habits in Action

Right in the heat of sexual intercourse, as well as when you're alone, regularly watch how your mind shifts in and out of fantasy gear. Especially, without judging yourself or trying to alter anything, make note of the automatic habits of your mind that shift you away from actual experiential reality with your lover and into past-future fantasies and thoughts. In this light, also make note of what the usual content of your fantasies are, and how these fantasies influence your sexual experience.

Establish Bodily Sensations
As Most Important

As we have seen, encounters with the mystic energies of the universe are not mental imaginings or daydreams; they are actual moments of communion with subtle realities that lie beyond personal consciousness and imagination. It is crucial that you learn consciously to direct your focus of attention toward where spiritual experience is to be found. This means focusing on the perceptual inputs that bring you into sensory communion with your lover—on touch and sound, seeing, smelling, tasting. Right at the sensory interface of your naked skin with your lover's naked skin, you will encounter the magic of mystic awakening. Right in the middle of perceptually encountering your lover through deep eye contact, the mystic powers can suddenly flood into your bodies and merge your separate realities into one greater being. And, of course, right in the middle of deep penetration of penis into vagina, the genital excitement can rush up through the whole body and awaken total mystic realization. By tuning into such pure sensations in the present moment, you open yourself to the sudden expansion of consciousness into deeper transpersonal encounter with your lover.

Nurture Your Breathing As
Your Reality Anchor

We have seen already that in order to silence your thinking mind, it is best at first to turn your full mental attention to your breathing experience. This same shifting of attention works miracles with transcending fantasy activity. Every time you remember to become one with your breathing, with the primal in-out flow of life-giving air through your nose or mouth, you effortlessly shift away from fantasy land and into the vastly more expansive and exhilarating reality land of transcendent intercourse with your lover.

Make the Present Moment All-Important

Fantasies are based, as we have seen, solidly in a past-future function of your mind. Therefore, they pull you off into a realm of reality that exists only in your mental processes. If you turn your magical power of attention to actual happenings in the present moment, you instantly free yourself from fantasy and pop your awareness into the living presence of the here and now. You come alive in the mystic dimension where the Spirit resides, and put yourself in a perfect position for experiencing transcendent communion with your lover.

Relax into the Intensity of Your Emotions

Practice the fine art of "breathing into" the excitement of being sexually awake in your body in the present moment. This is accomplished best by consciously taking breathers from the action of sexual relating. Our fantasy habits are usually linked with a pushing toward the future, toward more and more excitement and sexual release. To break this compulsive activity of the mind while making love, just pause and do nothing at all for a few breaths, so that you can concentrate on just "being" with your lover. Especially, let your exhales step by step discharge whatever emotional tensions you are holding in your body. By relaxing in the heat of passion, you will feel quite a remarkable sensation of bliss and contentment flood into you, and a new quality of sexual excitement will suddenly come into being.

Let the Spirit Move You

As this new energy floods into you, make no effort to further your sexual relating. Don't shift the mind into "what should happen next," because this will shift you into imaginings and memories—into thinking gear. Instead, just relax and enjoy doing nothing except sharing space with your lover. You will feel a new dimension of desire begin to come awake in your body as your awareness of your higher mystic self increases. Keep as primary your breathing experience, since it is through each new breath that the Spirit will enter your being. When thoughts and fantasies and future projections become quiet, suddenly your awareness of your body will amaze you; feelings you never had before will flood into you as your bubble of awareness effortlessly expands to include your lover. In this new level of communion, you will at some point spontaneously move into action again as your bodies and spirits continue the spontaneous sexual coming together that brings full ecstatic bliss and orgasm.

Stay Conscious All the Way

Every time you find yourself beginning to lose consciousness of the present moment, every time you slip toward fantasy or into thoughts to anticipate and control the sexual experience—again practice the fine art of pausing, of calming down to where you can sustain consciousness during the heat of passion. If you want your orgasm to be a radical spiritual experience, remember that you need to enter into the experience with your whole heart and mind and not drop away from expanded consciousness. Begin to gain some control over when you attain final orgasm, so that you can back off from this release experience when you want to, and prolong the sexual encounter long enough so that both of you attain the spiritual charge needed for full merging during orgasm. (I will speak much more of this in the following chapter.)

I have just outlined quite an intense long-term challenge for you to explore in your sexual encounters in the weeks and months to come. I'm confident that you'll find many pleasures opening up right from the very first time you remember, for instance, to keep aware of your breathing in the present moment when making love. Be gentle on yourself and don't try to discipline yourself into being spontaneous! Simply take on the challenge of remaining conscious of your own center, your own physical and spiritual presence, when you are heading for bed and in bed and in the arms of your lover.

To end this chapter, I want to share with you two experiential descriptions of what it can be like to apply these techniques to sexual situations. These two personal accounts are descriptions drawn from case studies where I asked clients to write down or talk into a tape recorder their realizations while following basic guidelines I have taught them about expanding their spiritual experience when making love. These two people you are about to get to know are man and wife, married for four years and with one child. They're not any part of the New Age movement, so they don't have any hip jargon to talk about their feelings. They're very much regular folks, and their honest reflections on their recent sexual experiences with each other are worth many chapters of psychological theory.

Beyond-Fantasy Confession One

RACHAEL: "I'm thirty-three, and I hate to admit it took me this long before I learned even the most basic things about really making love. When I was a little girl I think I instinctively knew how to dive into the intenseness of things in life, but somehow I lost that wild free feeling as I was growing up. It seems like almost everyone does.

"I actually started seeing a therapist for the first time in my life just a few months ago, not because I'm overly messed up inside myself but because my husband and I are making plenty of money these days and I heard from a girlfriend that there are certain ways to get more out of life. I'm not any kind of esoteric person but at the same time, I'm learning interesting things every day, and I'm always willing to try something new.

"I've been playing with some of John's suggestions and ideas for three months now. I feel like I'm just at the beginning, I'm not rushing myself. Everything takes time. But already things have changed, and that's partly because the idea came up in one of my therapy sessions that maybe I'd like to sleep alone some nights instead of always assuming I have to sleep with Richie. It's not that I don't love him, God knows I love that man. But there's some private part of me that just never gets breathing space. And besides, John says a lot of couples who are especially close and good in their sexual relationships have learned the trick of not sleeping together all the time. Otherwise the basic charge and attraction between two bodies gets lost.

"So for over two months now, Rich and I have been sleeping in different rooms, and this is a marvelous trick— sleeping alone most of the time makes me very quickly get charged to make love with Richie, like I used to when we first met. And it also gives me space to myself, just to be alone. God, I've been missing that feeling I used to have when I was a kid, you know, all alone, able to drift into dreamland, to have my own personal space. At first I thought Richie was going to just hit the ceiling when I suggested it, but he listens to reason, and imagine—he likes it too. Especially he likes how we feel again sexually. We were losing the charge, there was no doubt about that. Now we've got it back, or something new that's even better.

"But it's not only the sleeping apart bit. It's what we do when we're together. I've been talking this all over with Richie, every Thursday when I come home from my weekly session, we sit around at night and talk about what happened. Richie's an unusual man, that's why I'm with him. He's open to things like this. And when I give him an idea, he thinks about it, and we try it together sometimes, and that's what's made all this work so good.

"So this is how it works out. Now that I'm sleeping most of the time in the guest room, Rich and I don't just automatically slunch off to bed together. If we want romance, we have to come to each other and let each other know our sexual feelings. This has suddenly made us feel like lovers again instead of just a bored married couple. When things aren't taken for granted, life is much more intense. And that was what I was starting to lose in my feelings with Rich and why I went to a therapist in the first place. There are all these books about how to keep your love alive, but none of them quite made much real sense to me.

"Usually these last few weeks, I go in and lie with Rich anyway for a while before saying good night. Even if we don't have sexual energy, we find it good to cuddle up and enjoy each other's company. Sometimes we talk, sometimes we're quiet. Then later in bed alone, I'm completely in my own world for at least half an hour or so before I snooze off. It's amazing by the way how dreams get more intense when I sleep alone. But it makes sense. After all, I spent all my first twenty years of life sleeping alone, I know myself as a solitary sleeper and I love my solitary times.

"Last night when we got home from work and little Terry came over from Grandma's and we had dinner, I could tell that Rich was hungry for me. He gets this look in his eyes, and when I see what he's feeling, he can't keep a straight face. I like a man like that, who's not so subtle that you have to pry it out of him.

"Rich just takes off his clothes and jumps into the sack. I usually go into the bathroom and put in my diaphragm, and take my time getting undressed. That's becoming more and more of a special part of making love, too, when I'm alone with myself just before going to that man I love. By the time I walk out of the bathroom, I can feel my whole body already tight with passion. Usually I'm buzzing in my head in the bathroom, thinking a thousand things, remembering how it was last time with Richie, imagining what it's going to be like this time. I'm a real buzzer in my head that way. It's something I'm working on.

"Richie loves to see me suddenly walk into the room naked. I see it in his eyes. I was always shy deep down and sometimes still I feel shy. But now I can calm myself a little, and I like the rush of being shy and at the same time, when I meet Rich's eyes, I'm suddenly, well, I get hot and a crazy seductive feeling comes over me. I like to feel like a harlot sometimes. I think every woman does.

"Under the covers I go. Right at this point is where Rich is being a real male champion, because instead of being upset when I do something different, like when I just lie there and do nothing at first, he's interested in what I'm up to. I've told him a lot of what I'm thinking about and learning about concerning sex things and he's the kind of man who can just sit there with a curious look on his face and listen to what's on my mind, even if at first it's a little embarrassing to him. He just grins and makes funny comments, and then sure enough, he seems to be remembering what I told him, the next time we're in bed.

"So the last few times we've made love, we've both just relaxed beside each other for a minute or two at first. As soon as I start to listen to his breathing when I'm listening to mine, too, our breathing suddenly locks into the same rhythm. That's almost scary. It makes everything so intense. Then when finally one of us makes a move and reaches over to make contact, everything just gets more intense.

"Rich was always a fast guy, coming long before me most of the time. He's learning step by step now, though. He's learning not to get so tight and in a hurry, he's breathing into it all. And every time I feel him catching himself and slowing down, it's as if a hot flush comes through me, as if we make contact just—I can't describe the feeling but I love it, it's what love is. And I start to see it's a lifetime thing between two people; there's too much to discover in a lifetime. Every time we discover something, it opens up ten things more we never even knew were there. Subtle things I don't even have words for.

"Afterward we're sometimes able to talk about what we just felt. We're getting to the point where we're able to really tell each other about what we were thinking and feeling right in the middle of it all.

"Still, there's things I can't tell him yet. Like there's these great flashing moments that come to me more and more when he's inside me. I don't think I could ever describe them to anyone, they're simply beyond description. They're what orgasm is really all about for me more and more. I go for minutes on end in this place where I'm just not myself anymore. I'm not somehow emotional at all, I'm beyond what I used to think was emotion, unless bliss is an emotion. If there's a heaven, it must feel like that all the time."

Beyond-Fantasy Confession Two

RICH: "I'm not much good at sitting here alone trying to talk into a microphone. And I'm not much in the habit of talking about my personal sex life. But Rachael did it and I heard her tape just now, and what the hell, I'll give it a try. The truth is, I never know what Rachael's going to come up with next. This new sex thing's been a real twist. When she first told me she was going to go and see some therapist—I hit the roof is what I did. No woman of mine needs to go off and see a therapist. But Rachael, she has a way of putting things. Before I knew what was happening, the whole thing sounded perfectly okay to me. And it looks like she was right as usual. She's more adventuresome than me. I respect that in her.

"Here's the thing about sex. Everybody's got it. Half the people are busy flaunting it in your face and half of them are trying to pretend they don't have anything going on down below at all. But we're all packing a charge, that's what life is all about, and that's where Rachael's right. We got the energy. We should learn how to use it the best way we can. It's our pleasure center. It's a waste to waste it.

"I was brought up thinking that the men want it and the women mostly don't—they just go along for the ride because it's expected of them. That's how my momma was and still is, for all I know. But it didn't take me long to find out for myself that women like it, too. The thing is, I suspect they like it even more than we do, but it just takes them a while to get warmed up.

"I was always a wham-bam man without even realizing it back when I first got started. Those first few girlfriends of mine were real nice, never complaining about me jumping on them and then jumping off like a rooster. And even when I found out that they liked it slow, I was still pretty quick. I didn't know a guy could slow things down. I mean, nobody tells you anything about things like that, at least around my neck of the woods. I was brought up pretty lucky with money and things, but that didn't help much when it came to sex.

"It's like this with a male of the species. We grow up jerking off with our minds full of Playmates and *Penthouse* beauties and every other sort of picture we can get our hands on. I remember sneaking under the covers with my mags. But then, especially once I got a girlfriend or two, I'd shift over to remembering doing things with a girl, or imagining doing things, that was more like it the first few years. I had this strange sort of fantasy I don't think I want to talk about even though you say this is going to be confidential.

"The thing is, I was mostly in my head even when I was making out, there was this mixture of two things happening at once, the real live girl I was with and the fantasy girls in my mind. It was always a mixture. Rachael's been talking about this a lot recently, I never for a minute ever thought she was like me that way.

"The worst thing for me was this. Once I was with a girl for a while, I'd always sort of get tired of her. I wouldn't want to necessarily, but there it would be—the same old thing over and over again. So more and more, I'd play these fantasies through my mind when I was making love, imagining other girls I knew instead of the one I was with, or some actress from a movie—that's always haunted me, the way I can go to a movie and somehow fall in love or get hypnotized by some sexy broad on the screen, and have her showing up to fill up my imagination right in the middle of doing it with my girlfriend. Always I had these perfect beauties in my mind who were better looking and more sexy and all the rest than the woman I was with, so of course I'd imagine them when I was making love. It sounds sick when I talk about it now, but that's how it was.

"Then finally, just about when I was ready to give up on finding somebody to go the whole route with, along comes Rachael. There's a magic to life when it comes to things like finding the right woman, there's no doubt about that in my mind at all. Rachael struck me like ten movie actresses rolled up into one, at least that was how I saw her. She rang my bells and rang my balls at the same time. I was head over heels the first time she flashed me a glance, which was at work.

"At first, we tried to pretend nothing was going on be-tween us, because they don't like romances on the job. We're both doing pretty serious stuff these days that needs full concentration. But there was nothing we could do about it. Sex is one of those magnetic processes, I'm sure about that. Rachael got under my skin and I got under hers and we were like a couple of kids sneaking off together when nobody was looking.

"I had another girlfriend then, which made things compli-cated. I tried to toe the line and not let Rachael get to me. She tried to, too. But doesn't look like we succeeded, does it? And because at first we were hands-off, when we finally got down to it, there was sparks in the air, we could have lit a forest fire if we'd done it in the woods.

"But it didn't matter how much I loved her, still the fire died down after a while. She's a big thinker just like me, you know, she's off in her head as much as I am. That's what they pay us for at work, so when we come home, it's hard to turn it off. Half the time we'd be in bed doing it, and we'd be thinking about this thing and that at the same time. Just the last couple of months, she's been telling me about things like that, and we're damned similar, she's got her mind buzzing just as much as I do.

"What she's been learning at her therapy sessions scared me at first. Imagine what you'd feel like, for instance, if your old lady started telling you maybe it'd be best if she went and slept down the hall instead of with you—wouldn't you feel just one tiny bit defensive? But like I told you, she has a way of saying things that makes them just okay after a while, and she was right. What a woman!

"She's got me feeling like I felt right at the beginning with her, and it's not just from learning some new positions from some book or anything. It's like the inner game of tennis routine—it's all got to do with where you throw your attention when you're making it with the old lady. It's so simple, you'd think they'd teach it to us in grammar school. But it's not so simple to do when you get right down to it.

"Last night, for instance. I was lying there for what seemed like half an hour while she was in the bathroom. At first, I was being a good boy and trying to watch my breathing and fill up my body with my awareness, switch channels from thinking to feeling and all that stuff. But when she came walking into the room, I realized I was completely lost in a dozen thoughts at once. Then there she was, standing looking down at me, naked as the day she was born. She looked like a vision, like some goddess. She's always saying she's got to lose weight, but Jesus, she's perfect the way she is. Funny how women even when they're shapely keep thinking they should look different. The skinny girls all want to get fat, too.

"Rachael, she's sharp, she's already got figured out how

to change things in her head, and I can tell she's changing fast. You know what that means as well as I do, it means I'm up against the wall. I had a woman before who just took off into this new fad of working your hang-ups through and all the New Age stuff, and before I knew it, she was gone, she just left me in the dust. I was so busy at work, I didn't even hardly notice what was going on until it was too late. Now Rachael could do just the same thing if I wasn't experienced. But I'm going right along with her. I'm not going to get left in the dust this time. I mean if you don't trust the woman you're with and go along with her on this more subtle emotional stuff, then you're with the wrong woman anyway.

"The worst thing that happens is I get uptight and embarrassed sometimes, but nothing's come of that but good. Like last night, Jesus, she was telling me this amazing stuff about what she feels when I'm inside her. She's says she's riding rockets half the time and the other time she's just swinging low and easy until another rocket comes along and blasts right up her spine and then clear out the top of her head—that's what she told me. And I've got to confess, sometimes lately when I'm inside her, when we're doing it slow and sort of savoring the experience rather than trying to rush it, I get this feeling, like my whole body feels like my penis sometimes does. It's like a hundred, a thousand times more pleasure every time we do it than it used to be.

"There's this feeling in my chest and right in my brain too when I'm really hanging in there in the present and not getting off into thinking of fantasies or anything—and this feeling in my heart is as if I'm expanding in all directions, that's all I can say about it, except that it feels just very good, very good. It's relaxation, that's all it is, relaxation right in the middle of excitement, if you can figure that out.

"And right in the middle of the relaxation comes this

different kind of excitement—it's not even excitement, it's some sort of energy thing, or light, Rachael says it's a spiritual feeling and I guess if you want to think that sex can make you feel spiritual, then this feeling inside me is spiritual, although I don't think about it with that kind of words because for me spiritual things are church things, and I'm not altogether sure our minister would appreciate the association of singing hymns with what I feel when I'm on the inside of a sex rush. I feel like I'm some God myself, to be up-front about it. Sometimes I'm just blown off into—I don't know how to talk about it without sounding blasphemous.

"When I feel that way, the funny thing is that everything seems absolutely perfect. Especially Rachael seems absolutely perfect. There's just no desire to imagine being with some ideal sexy woman, because Rachael these days is that ideal woman. She gets just completely carried away, she's ecstatic—that's the word for it—she's not her usual thinking self. She's a vision, a complete living goddess. I don't even feel the push to come. I could just be right there deep inside her for days. She's shown me how to sit cross-legged and then she comes and sits in my lap, and that's just the perfect position for holding my charge. Lightening strikes, that's all I can say. But I can't hold still forever—I'm no Buddha— and pretty soon I feel this powerful urge welling up inside me and before I know it, without even thinking, I'm going into this animal feeling, and she laughs a special laugh that just provokes me more since I can feel she wants me to go animal, and I'm just pushing her down and there's no stopping it.

"Well last night was different, I have to admit. But I don't think I'm going to talk about that right now. All this talking's made me thirsty. I feel a little stupid sitting here talking to myself about all this. I hope I haven't just rambled on about nothing. All I can say is, I like where she's leading me, this present moment thing, that's where it's at. Who knows, maybe I'll make a Buddha after all and just sit there for a week with her in my lap. She says some people do it for a couple of hours at a time. That would really be something. Who knows what would happen. Just the few minutes that we manage these days is so much, I keep the feeling inside me for days afterward. And it's some sort of holy feeling if you ask me, but I don't think my minister would understand. These things I guess you got to keep to yourself. But anyway it's been interesting talking about it."

7

Mystic Orgasm

Lucy considered herself fairly well along the path to a fulfilling life. Her relationship with her husband was a good one and her three children were blessings to her in so many ways. But still there were certain things that she wasn't satisfied with, and one of them was her regular sex life with Ron. They could be so cuddly and close in the first phases of making love. But somehow toward the end, she found herself slipping away from the intimacy, afraid or unable to surrender her whole soul to the explosion of orgasm. She knew all the tricks to make herself come, that wasn't her problem. Her difficulty was in letting the orgasm carry her away into a deeper sense of mystic union with her husband. She'd had a few such spiritual experiences when making love, so she knew what was possible. But usually her mind played games with her and kept her caught up in her own little ego trips instead of setting her free to surrender to the truly magic realms of a full-blown transcendent orgasm experience.

The word *orgasm* has been bandied around so much in recent decades that sometimes it seems to have become a mundane thing, a topic for talk-show hosts to speak of as if they were speaking of any other bodily function. In truth, the orgasm experience is unlike any other human experience. As recent research has clarified, the orgasm is a phenomenal neurological happening in the brain—right in the middle of the pleasure center—that then floods the rest of the body with both a hormonal and an electrical rush.

Although certain theological circles would prefer it to be otherwise, more and more evidence points to the fact that the sexual pleasure center is one and the same with the bliss/ecstasy center of the human mind. The spiritual experience of mystic bliss and transcendent ecstasy seems to be almost identical to the total orgasm experience. Orgasm in a very real neurological sense appears to be the experience that weds body and mind, sex and spirit, into the ultimate human whole-body transfiguration.

I have thus far preferred to speak of the similarities between men and women in approaching the spiritual dimensions of sexual intercourse. As a couple delves deeper into sexual intimacy, differences between the genders do progressively fall away as spiritual realms become more dominant. When talking about the orgasm experience, however, it is vital for both members of the intercourse diad to understand intimately not only the similarities but also the differences between certain aspects of male versus female orgasm.

Toni Grant in *Being a Woman* stated the difference in quite blunt terms when she said that "orgasm for a woman is an opening up; in man, it is a spewing forth." There is no avoiding the reality that a man plays the crucial role of ejecting from his depths the precious male half of the procreation picture, while his female consort plays the equally crucial role of receiving that essence and providing the ideal inner environment for the sperm to swim a seemingly immense distance deeper and deeper inside her sexual realms until reaching the female egg and perhaps initiating the ultimate creative act of conception.

Always when making love, even of the most spiritual kind, this biological reality is in play, strongly influencing the experience that comes before, during, and after intercourse. To ignore or deny the earthly biological dimensions of intercourse is to short-circuit the basic energetic exchange between a man and a woman during sexual union.

We went through a period in the seventies and early eighties when men did their very best not to be brutes. Instead, they tried to be soft gentle lovers so that their partners wouldn't shout women's lib aphorisms at them. This experiment in consciously toning down the basic male aggressiveness in lovemaking proved to be quite a disaster, in certain ways, for everyone concerned. When men try to block their natural masculine feelings and to be feminine when making love, women usually end up hungering for more masculine toughness and assertiveness. And a man who is inhibiting his raw male energies when making love will be unsatisfied with the lovemaking, too.

In fact, any form of manipulation or repression of our primordial sexual instincts while making love leads to a lessening of the intensity of the sexual encounter. The last couple of decades have seen both men and women voraciously pouring over sex manuals that tell them how to manipulate the experience in order to improve their sex lives. The result has mostly been an even more severe fixation on thinking, thinking, thinking while making love, which stymies spontaneous interaction and certainly deadens spiritual awakening.

A book such as *For Yourself* by Lonnie Barbach, which promises to help you "take control of your life at its most intimate, personal and fundamental level—to achieve orgasm and a greater fulfillment of your sexual potential" might be of value in expanding a person's mental concept of what is possible during intercourse. But my experience in working with clients who have immersed themselves in such sex manuals and tried to apply them to their sexual encounters is this: Fixation upon technique, upon thinking about what to do next while making love, and controlling what one is doing moment by moment, directly thwarts true surrender of mind, body, and soul to the sexual encounter.

The problem with techniques designed to augment orgasm is that true mystic orgasm, as opposed to masturbatory orgasm, requires a sense of total abandon and surrender, a feeling of complete freedom from the very forms of mental functioning that sex manuals emphasize.

Men in the Act of Sexual Surrender

When the popular sex books, especially those aimed exclusively at the female market, aren't pushing orgasm technique, they are usually pushing the notion that women must learn to surrender to their men, to play the feminine role of passivity, so that the man can feel himself dominant and therefore satisfied in a monogamous relationship. Alexandra Penney pounds this attitude into print page after page in *Why Men Stray and Why Men Stay*. She actually makes such statements as, "Now you know the basic strategy to monogamy—feed-the-ego. You understand his basic ego needs: conquest, achievement, sex, power; and you recognize yours: love, loving and being loved. The second step is finding out what your particular man requires on a daily basis for care and feeding of his ego."

Thus the modern woman, in almost every book or magazine toying with the topic of male-female sexual relationships, is being programmed to believe that relationships are held together only by a crafty, creative, and often devious female who is tricky enough to manipulate a dumb hunk of an insensitive man into believing the dubious myth that he is the greatest guy in the world. Such low-level visions of what it means for a man and a woman to come together as one flesh completely ignore the vast and ultimately essential powers of long-term sexual attraction generated only through gaining a transcendent spiritual dimension in one's love life.

In the seventies, it was hip to say that there were really no differences between the sexes. Then in the eighties as the women's movement mellowed and backed away from its extremes, it became hip to make a big point out of certain extremes between the male and female psyche. Especially the commercial merchants of slick books and women's magazines played rather unfairly on women's fears of inferiority by trying to make women appear superior regarding relationship skills.

Now hopefully we are maturing in our understanding of sex similarities and differences to the point where we can put aside the glib and often psychologically invalid generalities we have been inundated with by the media. What seems important is that we learn to transcend gender differences where necessary to advance deeper into spiritual union, while glorifying gender differences where they are

essential in acting out the mythic dimensions of sexual relating.

The Fallacy of Female Surrender

It is certainly true that a woman must learn how to surrender
totally to a man if she is to attain a mystic merging of her
body and soul with his. But how foolish it is to forget to
mention that for there to be true spiritual union, the man
must do the same.

The simple truth of higher-level sexual relating is that
dominance simply cannot be a factor at all. In spiritual
realms of relating, equality is the essential foundation of all
dimensions of intercourse. Both men and women must learn
to surrender themselves not just to each other in any kind
of powerplay scenario but, more essentially, to the greater
spiritual force field that comes into play during lovemaking,
which unites their two beings into one infinite spiritual
presence.

At this level of sexual relating, there are no ego games
being played at all. That is the entire point. Spiritual orgasm
is a state of consciousness where personal ego is completely
although temporarily obliterated from the scene. And a
woman trying to feed her lover's ego while making love will
simply keep the sexual encounter at a low level of relating.
Instead of giving a man the freedom and space to relax his
ego-driven needs for dominance, she will be reinforcing this
ego mentality. The result can be nothing but frustration on
both sides, and very possibly a damaging of the relationship
because of the ego fixation.

I have of course been writing this book not just for

women, but for men and women equally. If you are a man reading this book, each time you do one of the sexual meditations we have been exploring, you are learning to surrender your ego dominance at a certain level. The male push for dominance and ejaculation is built into male genes, but it is not the only dimension of a man's personality. The actual spiritual quality that makes a man a man is his ability to relax his biological behavior and tune into a higher level of consciousness, where he is still a potent man, but not driven by his potency.

The *I Ching*, the great Chinese book of wisdom, does not recommend the nurturance of yielding for women only. In fact the thesis of the entire book is that the universe itself is based on an absolute balance between assertion and surrender, between power and love, between male and female energies. If anything, it is the man who needs to learn the fine art of surrender—but this does not mean surrender to his female counterpart; it means surrender of his own ego identity to his expanded sense of spiritual presence.

That's easy to say. And certainly both women and men need to learn how to surrender their egos while making love, and at many other points of friendship and intimacy as well. But how is it actually accomplished?

It's best accomplished, from my understanding, by using a particular "judo of the mind upon the mind." Instead of trying to force one's ego push for dominance into submissiveness by employing more ego games, it's wisest to give the ego new things to strive to accomplish other than dominance in the situation. Provide the assertive part of the mind with higher-level challenges to focus upon and master—such as learning to remain conscious of each new breath as it comes and goes, and expanding this awareness to include the heartbeat or pulse, the whole body in the present moment.

Everything you have been learning in this book thus far can be understood in this light of learning to transcend ego games and dominant/submissive patterns of the mind during sexual relating. The mind is a remarkably clever thing. Using low-level games to try to trick it into changing is not a wise game plan. Instead, as many psychologists and therapists have been learning during the last few decades, it is best to become grounded in the deep spiritual traditions of the world, where for thousands of years earnest observation has been made of how the ego functions, and how the ego can be gently, respectfully, and predictably shifted into a mode that encourages rather than blocks spiritual realization.

Each of the meditations and psychological exercises I have shown you thus far has been based on this traditional wisdom that knows how to merge normal consciousness with transformational consciousness. For instance, when you give your ego the challenge of remaining aware of your breathing experience even in the heat of sexual passion, you are offering your mind the direct opportunity to observe the basic balancing of male and female, the absolute equality between the receptive feminine inhale and the forceful masculine exhale. A person who is equally aware of each new exhale and inhale will naturally become balanced between assertion and submissiveness. Nature is the ultimate teacher of these primordial lessons.

Of course, the great mistake in sexual relating is that of thinking that a man is nothing but male energy and a woman nothing but female energy. A man must be willing to surrender part of his masculine presence in order to allow the woman to be assertive. Likewise, a woman must be willing to allow a man sometimes to become feminine and passive if a deep spiritual balance is to be found in the sexual relationship.

I remember being a wild young man, brought up on a cattle ranch to be a tough macho fellow, and then getting my first deep lesson of love from a sophisticated New York girl. "No, no," she said after allowing me to play constantly assertive bull with her without taking a pause to let her go into action. "Relax. Don't think you have to do all the work. It'll come of itself. Let me just take it out of you, you'll love the feeling."

In fact, perhaps the most definite sign of a mature man in bed is that he *does* know of the great transcendent shift into equality that comes when he stops being the assertive one all the time and just relaxes and lets the woman play the assertive role for a while. There is nothing more pleasurable for a man than that experience of relaxing and letting the power of the woman's internal energies effortlessly and not too quickly move the sperm from deep inside him out closer and closer to the point of no return. A man who surrenders his sperm in this way instead of forcing it upon the woman is a man who knows the sexual power in yielding to the feminine principle. Unfortunately, a woman who is trying to follow female sex books and let her man prove himself a man every time they make love is simply not being a whole woman, because women have a great deal of assertive masculine energy to express while making love. Sexual intercourse should always be a genuine balancing of male-female expressions for both sides of the erotic duo.

Lovemaking As a Team Effort

As long as lovers make the mistake of perceiving their sexual encounters as a feeding of egos and a manipulation of energies toward some mental or physiological goal, there will always be a compulsive sense of competition and battle in the erotic coupling of their bodies.

An exciting point at which ego-based sex turns into spiritual union is when two people suddenly realize that they are on the same team instead of feeling as if they are engaged in a one-on-one intimate-combat sport. Then they will be playing together toward a mutual desire for shared transcendence of all ego boundaries, for the awakening of that special feeling of love that can come flooding into their hearts, merging them through its transformational powers.

I have been speaking of the act of lovemaking throughout this book. It is time that we focus concertedly on what this big word *love* actually means in relationship to both sexual and spiritual relating.

Love most definitely refers to the sense of wholeness that is found not only in human hearts and sexual love but also in all manifestations of life and nature throughout the entire universe. Wholeness is the foundation of all religions. God is a concept that attempts to express the wholeness that binds everything together in the world. In saying that "God is love," the Bible clearly shows the ultimate definition of love.

Curiously, advanced scientists in the tradition begun by Albert Einstein are coming to the conclusion, as I mentioned earlier in passing, that the universe must be seen as an infinite, integrated, whole being in order for it to function at all. Something, some primal force, does hold everything together in the universe. Recently, biologists have even coined a word to describe the force that unifies all of life. The word is *autopoiesis* and is defined as "the maintenance of unity and wholeness while the components themselves are being continually and periodically disassembled and rebuilt, created and decimated, produced and consumed."

Specifically as this force manifests in human life, it is called love. Time marches on, lovers come and lovers go, civilizations rise and civilizations fall, but love remains eternal. The essential power that bonds two hearts as one is the energetic cement that makes human civilization possible.

Two human bodies are drawn together by the power of sexual love—this is certain. The basic force that holds families together is certainly this empathetic, compassionate force that pervades human civilization. Every culture, no matter how isolated from other cultures, has developed the concept of love as a primal dimension to its language. Love is a force that exists beyond human thought and philosophy. Our religions and sciences are simply trying to observe and make cognitive sense of a phenomenon that already exists.

What has been your experience with the power of love in your own life? Have you felt it directly, or is it just a concept to you? Can you surrender to this power, or do you fight against its influence in your life? Perhaps most to the point, do you bow down to this ultimate spiritual force, or is your heart hardened against holding ultimate reverence for it?

Take a breather and see what thoughts, feelings and intuitive insights come to mind, as you let your ego go to work at mastering the fine art of remaining aware of your breathing for a minute or two, while you expand this awareness beyond your ego domains and enter into truly spiritual reflection.

You Must Love Yourself First

For the orgasm experience to come into being at spiritual levels and not just masturbatory levels, both partners need first of all to have a deep sense of love for themselves. Then we can accept our lover just as he or she is. And through this acceptance, rather than through any attempts to manipulate oneself or one's lover, comes the effortless ability to open up to the inflow of spiritual love into a sexual relationship.

Thaddeas Golas has summed all this up in a remarkable little book that says vastly more than most sex manuals combined. Its curious title is *The Lazy Man's Guide to Enlightenment.* "In truth, a satisfying orgasm is a spiritual realization more than a technical accomplishment. The flesh is not apart from the spirit. A deep orgasm is a realization of love on many levels, including those which many of us now think of as 'animal.' Love, getting into the same space or the same vibration with others, is the ground of our being, and takes an infinity of forms. As in all other experiences, we always have the sexual experiences we deserve, depending on our loving kindness toward ourselves and others. But love is much broader than romantic passion, and it must begin with loving ourselves."

Loving ourselves is a two-edged sword of consciousness. First, we must love ourselves just as we are in all our imperfections, our ego trippings, our emotional inhibitions, our physical imperfections, and so on. At the same time, however, love requires that we see ourselves as perfect just as we are—that we see our godliness as holy creations in the universe, creations not needing any alterations at all in order to be seen as absolutely excellent and fulfilled.

Orgasm is a surrender of our egos on this crucial point especially—that we let go of all our ideas of being imperfect, of being limited, of being confined by our personal programmings and past histories and future projections. When a spiritual orgasm explodes in the mind and then radiates throughout the body, permeating the space around us and engulfing our lover in the process, we have attained a momentary state of perfect grace in the universe. This is the remarkable blessing programmed into our very genes—that we can, through sexual love, temporarily merge our personal consciousness with that of the Godhead and participate in the infinite love that animates all of life in the universe and beyond.

At this level, talking about a woman cleverly feeding a man's ego in order to hold a relationship together becomes pure poppycock. The power that holds a relationship together is love, not manipulation.

The most powerful psychic cement between a man and a woman is the generation of a mutual force field that encompasses the two separate bodies and minds. And this force field is generated most powerfully through sharing in the orgasm experience.

When you can say about your relationship that "we're a sexual team," then you know you've got something going for you. The power of love will generate the necessary adaptations and leaps of growth required by both of you in order to continue to play life together as a team sport. And the shared memory of recent orgasm experiences will serve regularly to put ego games in their place in your relationship.

Mutual Masturbation Versus Shared Orgasm

I remember that when I was twenty, people still spoke with a bit of reverence when they talked about orgasms. Men didn't talk about having an orgasm just because they ejaculated, for instance. Orgasm intrinsically carried a spiritual aura to it.

Recently, however, the male orgasm is often spoken of as a simple physiological happening, an experience that is the same every time, and that lacks the power and spiritual reverberations of a woman's orgasm.

In actual fact, as Masters and Johnson showed through EEG brain-activity studies several decades ago, the orgasm experience for human males is a highly complex neurological affair. It is quite different from other animals as a neurological happening, and never the same twice. The same person, even when making love with electrodes attached to his head, will exhibit radically different electrical activity from one orgasm to the next.

An honest male masturbator can attest to this fact quite readily. Sometimes the process of bringing oneself to ejaculation or orgasm is experienced as no big thing. A reasonably talented man, for instance, can bring himself to ejaculation in less than a minute, and feel almost no rush in the brain at all in the process. Similarly, women can masturbate and have a low level of explosion in the pleasure center of the brain. At other times, both can reach orgasm and have white lightning strike down their spines.

Making love for real is just the same, only more so. The experience of coming can be mundane or transcendent. The brain may barely register the energy discharge, or it may remain in white light for minutes on end, even for much longer periods of time if actual Tantric or Kundalini sexual meditation is being practiced by experienced lovers.

The majority of us learned about activating our sexual pleasure center in the brain through self-stimulation alone in bed as we mastered the masturbation process. There is no denying the spiritual importance of masturbation. "Masturbating was when I first discovered that there's a place I can go where I'm beyond myself," one client explained. "I don't think I would have survived spiritually through my teen years if it hadn't been for my regular jerk-off sessions. The term is a rather crude one, but the experience for a teenage boy can be so, so lifesaving. I discovered through masturbating that I can become pure pleasure, pure bliss. I found a dimension to myself that I could love without reservation. I would have to admit that I first learned about the magic of meditating by masturbating."

Masturbation is also a discharge process that can be used not for spiritual expansion but simply for the release of negative tensions that have built up during the day. Sex certainly is a masterful therapeutic tool in this regard. We can release our daily tensions either through masturbation or sexual intercourse. This is a great emotional boon to humankind.

The problem with this is that we can become addicts to the quick-discharge routine. We can come to identify orgasm with just the lower dimensions of coming. These habits, usually established in teen years, often stand directly in the way of true spiritual orgasm, as we have been seeing throughout this book.

The beginning step in seeing whether this is true in your own life is simply to follow the golden transformation rule of observing yourself when making love the next few times, and remembering making love the last few times. Are you in fact engaging in transformational intercourse, or are you simply engaging in mutual masturbation? Specifically, does your heart become awakened through sexual arousal and climax, or do you remain down at a mostly genital level of excitation and discharge?

Pause and let yourself look back and reflect on this key question, not to judge yourself but simply to see and accept yourself.

The Hard-Wiring of the
Male Sex Drive

We need to delve deeper now into what constitutes the full range of human orgastic potential. At the genetic baseline is the procreative fact that men definitely need to ejaculate in order to get their swimmers into female territory. Nature has made this ejaculation experience highly pleasurable in order to reinforce the ejaculatory behavior. Nature has also hard-wired male brains to be aroused by the proverbial ass and tits visual stimulation as a prelude that pushes the buttons for attaining the pleasure of ejaculation. At this level, men are similar to their mammalian cousins.

As an example of how preprogrammed we actually are in sexual preferences and behavior, recent research exploring the origins of homosexual behavior in men has offered extremely important results.

Beginning with rats, as is often the case in research, it has been ascertained step by step that if a pregnant woman undergoes extreme stress during pregnancy, the likelihood of her child being homosexual is quite high. Perhaps the most significant research in this regard has been that of Gunter Dorner, director of the Experimental Endocrinology Institite at Humboldt University in East Berlin.

In the early sixties, Dorner began his work by establishing that definite endocrine differences exist between homosexual and heterosexual men. During subsequent years, he did extensive interview and questionnaire studies that established that mothers of homosexual men suffer from vastly greater incidents of high stress during pregnancy than those of heterosexual men. "About a third of the homosexual men and their mothers reported having been exposed to severe maternal stress—such as bereavement, rape or severe anxiety," he reported. "And about another third reported moderate stress. This wasn't true of the heterosexual men. None of them reported severe stress. And only ten percent reported even moderate stress. As a result, I am forced to conclude that male homosexuality is the result of permanent neurochemical changes in the hypothalamus effected by reduced levels of testosterone during fetal life. The tissues, neural circuitry and chemistry of the brain have already been stamped during fetal life by the sex hormones. The foundations have already been laid, before birth, for the range of behaviors that will characterize the organism as male or female in adult life."

Although all scientific findings remain open to moderation and even reversal, it does seem quite probable that we cannot really choose what our basic sexual preferences and feelings will be in life. Our challenge in becoming mature sexual beings is in fully accepting and appreciating the hard wiring in our brains regarding our sexual hungers and behavior, while also learning step by step to evolve beyond our initial compulsive relationship to our sex drives. We can fulfill our manifest destiny as unique individuals, even though we cannot alter our basic neurological wiring that makes us who we are. This is another reason why we must come to love ourselves just as we are if we are to then expand our experience of who we are to include deeper spiritual dimensions of consciousness.

In like manner, it does appear that men are prewired to crave the sex act, to actively hunger for and seek out opportunities for ejaculation, and to do this oftentimes just to relieve genital pressures that have built up, and to enjoy the physiological pleasures that come through having sex. This basic genetic programming makes men more compulsive about sex than women, and through the ages has caused great conflicts and emotional suffering between couples. A man feels hungry for sex in and of itself, as a genetic urge. What is he to do about this definite hunger when his culture, his religion, and certainly his wife are often bothered by it?

Luckily, men also have the essential quality of transcendence built into their genes, enabling them to take their raw sexual charge and channel it in a variety of worthwhile and stimulating directions. It is, as Joseph Chilton Pearce has pointed out in *Magical Child Matures*, the primary charge of sexual energy in the human body that actually serves to motivate and activate all our various activities. The inherent power of our drive to have sex and procreate is the underlying energy that moves us in all our actions.

This realization lies at the heart of Sigmund Freud's psychological understandings, as well as in the more spiritual understandings of the various world religions that employ sexual energy for spiritual awakening.

We all are born with the primal urges to survive, to procreate, and to enjoy life as much as we can in the process—such is the human situation. For men constantly packing the physiological pressure to release sperm and in the process enjoy the ejaculatory pleasures, this means that we take our raw sexual energies, we appreciate our mammalian urge to have sex with whatever women we encounter who attract us—and we learn as we mature how to channel our great outflowing of ejaculatory energies in many different manifestations that satisfy us.

Especially when it comes to sex, we learn how to deepen the orgasm experience into mystic realms that blast us beyond the lower-level programmings of our mind and into vastly more fulfilling realms. The fact that it takes many years of making love with the same woman to explore fully this spiritual dimension of sexual relating quite naturally tends to make us mostly monogamous. We don't have to try to violate our natural sexual desires in order to offer a woman the relationship for which she is also hungering.

The Female Orgasm

Throughout the world, male dominance has been rampant in most civilizations, often to the point of abject brutalism and degrading subservience of women. Our society has been at least partly transformed through the gallant efforts of a certain group of activist women who fought the good fight for equality and reality-based relating between men and women. But all extreme movements, by the laws of nature, must learn to seek the balance of moderation or fizzle into obscurity. My observation has been that women have been remarkably mature in quickly seeking a balance point for their ongoing struggle for equality and fairness between the sexes.

The anthropological reality behind the entire battle between the sexes that has been raging recently seems to be that for countless thousands of years during the hunter-gatherer period of human life on this planet, which came to an end just four to six thousand years ago, there was definitely a gender factor in the separation of work roles and family responsibilities. Quite simply, the men tended to do the hunting and the women the gathering. The men were the ones who went out and struggled with the environment and brought back the game while fending off aggressors, while the women provided the nurturing environment for raising the new generations, and kept the more delicate psychic dimensions of human community alive and flourishing.

The present differences in male and female bodies reflect

this difference in natural roles. The similarities between male and female bodies are certainly far more extensive than the differences, which means that men can definitely take over many of the traditionally female roles in society, and women are certainly able to take on the male roles. Definite differences, based primarily on the opposite sexual roles of man and woman in creating and bearing the young, do exist, however. A woman's body is different from a man's body, and this difference needs to be openly accepted and integrated into our understanding of sexual relating.

What does this mean in a sexual relationship, and, especially, how are women different from men at the level of orgasm? First of all, as zoologist David Barash has pointed out in *The Anatomy of Sex and Power*, by Michael Hutchison, "There is no compelling evidence for a female orgasm in any animal other than Homo sapiens." A female in other species comes into heat and broadcasts her readiness for insemination, and then the sexual response of the male and his assertiveness usually force the issue toward the needed ejaculation of the male into the female.

There is not very much pleasure involved in this mating process, when compared with the human potential for pleasure while making love. And this seems especially true for the females of nonhuman species—they tend to get gang-banged whether they are enjoying the experience or not. And clitoral stimulation seems to be almost nonexistent. "The female orgasm probably doesn't occur in a natural state among most mammals because the clitoris doesn't receive sufficient stimulation in the usual intercourse and love play of most mammals," Dr. Helen Singer Kaplan has stated. "The clitoris receives little stimulation since mounting is usually from the rear."

In the same way that men have nipples that serve no direct purpose in their male lives, the clitoris has no functional purpose—except to provide pleasure, sometimes immense pleasure.

It is often said that the female orgasm is of much greater neurological amplitude than that of the male, because for the female, the explosion is purely internal, whereas for the male, it is released in physical discharge.

"When I come," a female client reported in this regard, "it seems as if for minutes on end I'm in bliss, transported into oblivion and beyond into this remarkable state where I don't exist but at the same time I'm infinitely gigantic and just one great pulsating white-light presence. For my husband, he blasts off inside me and then quite quickly the whole thing is over for him; he returns to normal and doesn't share with me in the lingering aftermath of orgasm. I feel like I get ten times the pleasure that he does from coming. He discharges his energy into me, and I pick up his energy on top of my own—that's how it feels to me. I think women get the best deal that way, if they get to come at all."

It seems to take the average woman about twenty minutes of intense sexual encounter and stimulation before the orgasm reflex comes into play and transports her. I know women who often come after ten to twelve minutes of sexual relating, and some who need much longer than twenty minutes, so we shouldn't set the alarm clock on twenty minutes and expect to perform in accordance with the linear flow of time.

Still, usually it takes a woman much longer to reach orgasm than a man, since men can go from relaxed genital condition to ejaculation in about one minute with proper stimulation (Masters and Johnson). Why is there this difference, if our sexual behaviors have evolved out of a logical set of survival pressures?

Perhaps the best way to see this, as Michael Hutchison

has pointed out in *The Anatomy of Sex and Power*, is through the following logic. It would be counterproductive if the woman came before the man did, and terminated intercourse before the seed was planted. If the woman was satisfied and got up and left before the male could plant his sperm, procreation would certainly suffer. So the timing seems well intended in this regard.

Furthermore, it is important that active intercourse end after twenty minutes or so. Otherwise, if pleasure continued for hours on end, there would be little energy left over for other things in life, such as hunting and gathering. By ending the sexual bout after plenty of time has been allowed for the average male to ejaculate, a healthy, efficient balance of sex and other activities is ensured. In short, "evolutionary forces have selected for women who have the capacity of being rewarded with an orgasm, but who don't have their orgasm more quickly than the male."

When one speaks in this way about the human system sexually, one is talking about the basic survival of the species. One is not talking about the higher dimensions, the more subtle and spiritually potent ones where basic reproduction of the species is taken care of at the same time that additional important aspects of human life are also encouraged.

Without a doubt, the bonding that happens between male and female during orgasm serves both to keep father and mother together to care for the young and to provide the emotional foundation for sharing spiritual communion with each other. The biologists, of course, do not speak in public about the possibility that spiritual communion helps to keep the species thriving. But in private, I have had many many such discussions. By and large, biologists are not often dogmatically religious, but they are almost always deeply mystical and spiritual in their more private lives. It is in fact almost impossible to look at the miracle of life on this planet of ours and not feel reverent, in awe, spiritually swept away by the reality of life itself.

This seems to be the heart of the orgasm experience—getting swept away into the immensity of life itself, through gaining direct experiential access to the primal power of love that pervades life. When we make love, we actually do make something through our shared passions. Something new comes into being. We raise a charge higher and higher in our bodies until the charge ignites an explosion that consumes our egos, that burns our tensions up into nothingness, that blows a hole in our conceptually limited sense of who we are, and lets the breath of God come over our senses, blowing gently like a springtime breeze into our inner realms of consciousness.

Certainly we can experience such transcendence at lower levels of intensity in many other spheres of life. Orgasm is not the only vehicle for consciousness expansion by any means. It is just the most thrilling, the most intense, the most readily available path to temporary enlightenment. It is also the path that we can walk most intimately with a friend. Most meditation is a very solitary affair. Sexual meditation is like having our cake and eating it, too. It is both immensely internal and at the same time remarkably transpersonal.

Dr. Helen Singer Kaplan has stated that "female orgasm is an artifact from the point of view of evolution. In other words, we could have survived successfully as a species without female orgasm, but we could not have survived without male orgasm. From an evolutionary standpoint, the female orgasm is a luxury."

This implies that all of spiritual experience is a luxury, not a necessity in human life. This is almost certainly not a true statement, however. None of our world civilizations would have flourished if we had remained fixated on the lower genetic realms of consciousness. Perhaps our species as a physiological presence would have survived, but the depths of the human experience would certainly have withered up and died without the spiritual dimension present throughout the ages.

In sum, the presence of the female orgasm does three things that seem essential to our human civilization. First of all, it awakens a level of intense love in the heart of the woman that then encourages the man to reach this level of spiritual orgasm himself, so that there is a bonding between mates. Secondly, the female orgasm offers the woman herself direct access to her deeper spiritual realms of personal consciousness. And thirdly, the female orgasm makes sex a fair-game, equal-pleasure experience rather than a male-dominated affair.

It seems a reasonable assumption to say that the heightened understanding of the female orgasm has been one of the most powerful agents for positive change in the last century. Instead of men taking their pleasure from women without thinking of the woman's pleasure, women are now insisting on their equal rights to pleasure while making love. This valid demand has had an immense positive effect on the level of consciousness of contemporary men.

Especially, the male ejaculation experience has been transformed by sharing space and pleasure with the female orgasm. Men are finally gaining access to the spiritual dimensions of orgasm by learning to slow down and go more deeply into their own sexual charging experience while awaiting the charging and then the magnificent discharging of their female counterparts.

"At first I tried to stay hard longer just out of guilt," explained one man regarding his experience. "I felt guilty when I came and she didn't get to. But step by step, I started to really get into the holding-back part of making love. It's the difference between just chugging a bottle of hundred-dollar wine right from the bottle as fast as you can to get a buzz on and sipping the wine slowly with an intimate friend, spreading the pleasures out over a longer time so that the enjoyment can really be felt. Somehow when I take my time now in bed, I get more alive all over my body. It's one of those clichés, I'm learning how to make love with my heart and not just my balls. That's the big step I've made in my love life, and it took time. But I had a good teacher recently."

The Kundalini Lover

In the ancient Yogic tradition of Kundalini meditation, there is an amazing tradition that uses the instinctual sexual energies of the nervous system as the primary vehicle for awakening spiritual realization throughout a person's being.

The Yogic masters discovered through centuries of deep inner meditation that there are in fact seven different energy centers in the body, with the sexual energy center being one of them, lying at the base of the spine. In puberty, the sexual center becomes activated with the power of creation itself—the divine spirit enters the human body and resides in the genitals, ready from an evolutionary point of view to fuel the action that will lead to the creation of new human life on the planet. This part of the story runs roughly parallel with the bioevolutionary view of sexuality we explored in brief a few pages earlier.

What the ancient masters discovered through meditation, through using the power of attention to observe the mind and body intimately in action, was that the sexual energy center is intimately connected with higher energy centers that lie up high along the spine and in the brain itself. The center of willpower, for instance, lies in the belly region of the body, and sexual energy can rise up into the will center, turning a person into a powerhouse of action.

Higher up in the chest is the heart center, or chakra, where sexual energy becomes transformed into the power of love. In basic terms, if a person, man or woman, has an orgasm without the heart's center being awakened in the process, then the experience has been masturbatory, a release of genital energy but not an awakening of love and compassion.

It takes time during arousal for the sexual energy to rise up into the heart center. Very possibly, this is related to why it can take a woman twenty minutes to achieve full orgasm: The sexual excitement must spread upward and reach the heart before true orgasm is attained.

Once the heart is awakened in lovemaking, from the Kundalini point of view, there are even higher realms of consciousness that can be awakened by raising the sexual energies up from their genital fixation. In the throat is an energy center related to the ability to communicate, to think clearly, to express one's inner feelings with words.

Many times people are stuck in this thinking center of the body when they start making love. So actually, as we have seen, we often first have to shift our energetic focus down from the head to the genitals in order to tap into the power of sexuality—and then bring the energy back up, transforming it as it passes through the heart.

Above the thinking center is the intuitive center—the third eye as it is often called—which is located between the eyebrows in the pituitary center of the brain. When, during sexual arousal, you suddenly feel bliss and light entering your being, it is because this region is being activated by the sexual charge rising up from your genitals. Great flashes of intuitive insight often come through activating this center, as well.

Finally, there is the energy center called the crown chakra, which lies at the top of the head. During orgasm, it is here that connection is established with transbody spiritual energies, so that sudden expansions of consciousness can occur. Not only does energy flow up and out through this top energy center. Energy also comes flooding into the body from above in total spiritual orgasm.

The optimal energetic condition from the Kundalini point of view is when sexual, earthly energy rises upward in the body at the same time that heavenly, spiritual energy flows downward into the body. When these twin flows of energy (heaven being usually seen as masculine and earth as feminine) encounter each other in the middle of the energetic system (the heart) and fuse together, true orgasm occurs. At this point, all the energetic centers are activated in an ultimate flash of white light and union with the Godhead.

This Kundalini model is an advanced conceptual framework that attempts to describe an experience that is beyond concepts. The importance of this model for our present discussion is that it encourages us to focus our attention consciously on allowing the genital charge of energy we feel during sexual arousal to rise up through each of these higher energy centers I just described. This is the true spiritual path to using orgasm energy for attaining temporary enlightenment while making love.

The book *Sexual Secrets* states that "the conscious awakening of Kundalini-power requires strength of mind, awareness of the natural evolutionary upward movement of this raw sexual energy, and a physical body in harmonious balance." It goes on to say that "sexual contact is particularly liable to stimulate and awaken the Kundalini within. Lovers sometimes experience Kundalini spontaneously, through the convergence of life energies during love-making. If the Kundalini is awakened through spontaneous, joyful love-making, it offers the couple a great opportunity to explore the heights of the spirit."

What I have been doing in this present book is exploring the most pragmatic ways to encourage this awakening of the deeper spiritual dimensions of sexuality, without employing the particular religious jargon and esoteric techniques to be found in the Kundalini tradition. The awakening of upward-rising spiritual energies in the sexual experience is a natural experience. Meditation techniques can augment this development, but the potential for spiritual awakening through sexual intercourse can be tapped into without formal meditative training.

It has often been said in one way or another that the difference between a man and a woman is that a man comes with his balls and a woman comes with her heart. From the Kundalini point of view, this is very often a true statement. A man has such a physiological drive to ejaculate, the pressures are so constant and powerful to have genital discharge, that a man's habitual genital fixation when coming is quite understandable. Solitary masturbation routines of boys while in their teens, as we have seen, account for much of this genital conditioning.

Women on the other hand do not have this physiological spermatic pressure to come. Their entire experience of sexual arousal is therefore usually more of a whole-body experience. "I'm actually one of those women who never really got into masturbation much," one friend told me. "I was always more of an emotional person than a sensation type, I guess. I have to get touched here in the heart before my genitals wake up. And coming isn't so much a clitoral experience for me, sure there's the sensation down there, but even though it might sound strange and I've never said it aloud before, I feel like I come in my heart, and right up through the top of my head, more than down between my legs. And after I come, it's my entire body that's afire, that's tingling, that's alive with the aftermath of it all. It's like I'm electric and solid at the same time, it's impossible to describe. And when I totally open my heart to my husband when he's inside me, I feel he's me and I'm him, there's no separation at all, and this feeling lingers for hours afterward, sometimes for days on end. That's the magic of orgasm for me. We only make love once a week or so but that's plenty. We build up a good charge and then let it blast us off together. That's what we've learned from twenty years of making love together. It's part of our way to stay sane in this insane world. At least in the middle of orgasm, everything makes sense and everything's okay, more than okay, perfect just the way it is."

Come Together Right Now

A great mystique has arisen in recent years regarding the essential requirement that the man and the woman come together at the same time. Many men have agonized over trying to keep themselves from coming too soon, and many women have agonized over not being able to come in time to do it with their lover. We've already discussed several times the positive value of a man learning to slow down his ejaculation speed so that his partner can come too. But is it essential for spiritual bonding that sexual partners reach orgasm at the same time?

My opinion on this is that couples make a great mistake

when they place too much importance on the shared orgasm. Shared orgasms are orgasms in which both parties
are conscious and participating in the energy of orgasm.
They are not necessarily simultaneous events. "At first Jack
would come after just a few minutes into intercourse," one
client told me. "It was frustrating for me of course, but I
didn't complain because I loved him so much in other ways.
I'd just not have an orgasm some of the time. That wasn't
so bad. I can live without orgasms, to be quite honest.
They're not the center of life for me. But as the years went
by, Jack and I got to where we could talk about sexual
things, and he started to hold himself back, and to be more
aware of me wanting to come. Then after he heard a lecture
at the university on Chinese techniques for withholding the
semen, he started something new, which was actually pulling his penis out of me a few times while we were making
love, so that the constant stimulation wouldn't make him
come so quickly. I let him know that it didn't bother me
when he pulled himself out. He'd had a girlfriend before
me who got upset when he did that—imagine, it took four
years before he found out I preferred to have him pull
himself out sometimes and relax a little. It gave me more
time, and somehow it made lovemaking more exciting to
pause like that, to take a breather, not to be just so hot and
bothered all the time. But then he got to where he was
holding himself back so much, it was too much. I'm one of
those women who likes to come after the man has come
anyway, I've read that there's lots of women like me. Somehow I need Jack to come in order to push me the final step,
you know. I'm still shy after all these years to come before
him, and the couple of times I came with him at the same
moment, well to be quite honest it was strange somehow,
we were so caught up in our own comings that we were
hardly aware of each other. Now I just tell Jack go ahead

and come honey, when I feel him really ready, and then he just enjoys himself tremendously, and I'm right there with him when he comes. I can feel him spraying inside me, I swear to God I can. Then he's just lying there and I get this special feeling, like I've got all the time in the world, like the pressure's off now that he's come, and the amazing thing is that I've found that as his penis gets slowly smaller and smaller, I can work myself against it and get a finer and finer feel, you know, and if I don't come before, I come just as he slides out of me. That's like paradise, that is. I just can't keep myself from crying out, and sometimes he gets excited again when I come and there we are really caught up in something delicious going on like it's going to go on forever."

Most men can in fact quite easily prolong their sexual potency in bed, at least to a certain extent, even without using any special Kundalini techniques. There are three key ways to do this. Let me list them clearly, in case this is something you want to explore in depth with your lover.

First of all, remember that tense breathing leads to premature ejaculation, and deep breathing, especially slow exhales and plenty of time spent empty of air at the bottom of each exhale, enables a man to take his time in coming. By focusing on the breathing, there is also a natural focusing on the heart region and on feelings of compassion. The shifting from genital fixation to heart focusing brings the energy up from the balls and into the heart, which, as we saw from the Kundalini understanding of sexual meditation, is one of the crucial ways of both prolonging and amplifying the spiritual dimensions of lovemaking.

Secondly, as I'm sure you know from experience, the less stimulation to the penis and balls, the longer a man can sustain his pressure without coming. This doesn't mean, though, that a woman should keep hands and lips off. In fact, one of the ways of prolonging erections is for the woman to learn how to bring just a little bit of semen out of the penis to release the intensity of the pressure without the whole shot getting spent. Learning to do this is one of the pleasures of love for both involved. Most men think that it's all or nothing, but this is simply not the case.

Oral sex is of course one of the best ways to prolong sex, if done in the right spirit. Certainly the amount of time a man is down on a woman expands the time spent with an erection, and also aids the woman greatly in reaching orgasm. There is a special feeling in the genitals and entire body when a man is down on his knees between a woman's spread legs, paying homage to her mystic female opening into the realms of human creation.

This, of course, is where making love is the same as doing yoga—in fact, every posture when making love, when done with whole-body awareness and relaxation right in the middle of the tensions, is sexual yoga. The key point is not to hold one position too long. Keep letting your bodies move spontaneously into new positions; this will expand the time spent in lovemaking effortlessly.

The third thing, as we just saw, that helps greatly in prolonging an erection is the primal act of removing the penis from the vagina on a regular and ritualistic basis so that too much stimulation doesn't provoke ejaculation. Once a man and a woman start truly working as a team in this regard, the comings and goings from the vagina are great pleasures.

Most women I have spoken with about this say they love the coming-and-going sensations and emotional provocations just as much as they love the constant inside action. There are so many subtle ways for the penis to stimulate the clitoris, and exploring regular comings and goings in different postures is the best way to expand clitoral stimulation while at the same time prolonging intercourse.

Positions in this regard are important, if explored spontaneously and not mechanically. For instance, studies show that a man comes most quickly when lying on top of a woman, both because this is probably his conditioned masturbatory position and because gravity does take its toll, pulling the sperm down and out. With the woman on top, however, things progress much more slowly. The man can relax his whole body and doesn't have to play into the dominant aggressor role so much—although sometimes toward the end this is certainly the preferred experience for both involved.

The Kundalini position of Yab-Yum, where the man sits cross-legged and the woman sits in his lap with her legs around him—is the way to stay erect the longest. It is a position where both people can remain calm without moving for long periods of time, feeling the sexual energies rushing up and down the spine, indulging in the spiritual dimensions while the orgasm energy rises more and more up the spine into the higher energy centers.

At this point, sometimes the man can choose not to come at all, if he believes the Kundalini and Taoist teachings that conserving the sperm preserves potency, which is quite possibly true. Otherwise, through subtle movements of male and female bodies, the sperm will rise up like a volcano, and orgasm for the woman can come like a great shower of holy light throughout her nervous system as the two bodies merge in pure light.

Men like me, of course, brought up on a cattle ranch and still cowboys deep down, still prefer sometimes to finish things with the wild haystack fling, and I suppose it's only natural that men like me find themselves with women who like that, too. A balance between the spiritual and the animal—a total awakening of both—seems the ultimate in sexual intimacy, where genitals come afire, hearts melt, spirits soar, and souls merge into one infinite, vitalized being.

You certainly must have your own story to tell regarding your experiences of the dimensions of lovemaking we have been exploring in the preceding pages. Take some time now away from reading if you so choose, so that you can reflect on what works best for you when making love, and also consider your present relationship with your personal orgasm experience and that of your lover—and consider directions you might want to evolve in as the next days and weeks go by.

8
Sexual Communion

John and Christa knew that they were blessed with a beautiful sexual relationship. During their three years together, they'd explored all seven of the dimensions of spiritual intercourse that we have now discussed in this book. They both felt deeply fulfilled with each other sexually. What confused and sometimes upset them was how they often felt right after a passionate spiritual union during lovemaking. It seemed to both of them that the deeper they plunged into spiritual consciousness during sexual intercourse, the more they sensed that some sort of new being was being created and nurtured by their lovemaking. They didn't know how to relate to this mystic feeling. Did it mean that they were perhaps ready to have a baby, or was there some other explanation for their feelings?

It is only natural and to be expected that as lovers come closer together emotionally, physically, and spiritually, they wake up within themselves a feeling of shared creation, of procreative potency. In fact, I would venture to say that it is virtually impossible to be spiritually expansive while making love without encountering at some point the mystic muse of creation.

But how are we to respond to these procreative feelings and thoughts that often rise up in the aftermath of a beautiful sexual experience? Are we to assume that our lovemaking must inevitably lead to the creation of a baby, are we just to ignore these feelings, or are there other ways to respond to postorgasm procreative visions?

First of all, let's survey the different feelings that often do arise right after making love. This is a topic I regularly bring to light with clients during therapy sessions, since it can raise to the surface of consciousness so many different psychological processes happening deep within a person's mind and soul. Here is a fairly representative sampling of the various responses I have received from people when I asked them about their postcoital feelings.

"I end up after coming with my whole body supercharged," a twenty-four-year-old man named Jacob, who plays in an up-and-coming country-jazz band, told me a couple of years ago, "and usually I can hardly stay in bed. I jump up as soon as it's allowable, you know, as soon as my girlfriend won't get her feelings hurt, and I get my guitar and go to work on some new tune; that's when I'm most hot writing songs, when I've just made love."

Another man, fifty-two years old, just married for the third and he hopes the last time, said, "I have a different feeling recently. It used to be that I'd feel just totally blown away and go mostly unconscious, hardly knowing or caring where I was after coming. I'd start the lovemaking bout feeling nervous and hungry and pushy to come, and then once I fired off, I'd do a fade routine, feeling nervous some- how about being with the woman. I'd just pass out, or I'd immediately have to start talking, or I'd just get up and jump back into gear. Now with Gabriella, I've finally found some sort of peace in making love, I can come and then just do nothing, just lie there in her arms or side by side and indulge in the emotions rushing through me. It's a paradise feeling that comes over me these days, and I must say it was worth pushing for all these years to attain, although I can't say I actually did something to attain it. I'd have to say it came as some sort of grace to me, after all those years of feeling somehow empty and unsatisfied after making love. And all I can say is that it's because I'm really in love this time. I'm more than in love, I'm, well, I'm satisfied. So I can relax into it."

A young woman named Jennifer, during a recent sexual- intimacy workshop, shared the following details regarding her experiences while making love. "It all depends on how Doug takes me," she said to the group, blushing slightly but feeling brave enough to speak openly. "If he's really present, if he hasn't been drinking, for instance, and if he isn't thinking about some business problem, then when he comes, everything depends on whether he's waited long enough so I can come, too. If I don't come and he does, I'm embarrassed to take my pleasures upon him—you know what I mean—and so I fake being satisfied and not needing to come, and that's pure hell. And recently he's off on busi- ness trips so often, he's making so much money these days— and I'm home alone, so at some point I have to be satisfied bringing myself off, but it's not the same as with him. There's really no comparison. Sometimes when he's in just the right mood, I can lead him along so that I get time to get ready. I've learned so many things that he likes me to do to him, and he's getting more into doing things to me too, so we're learning. And when he's slow and loving with me, when he's focused on me and I can feel him building like a powerhouse inside me, then at a certain point I just go crazy under him, and sometimes on top of him too. I'm not as bashful as I used to be. Then when I come and he comes, it's pure celestial bells ringing in my ears for minutes on end, and I feel him so close, I feel our hearts so close, and then this feeling comes up inside me—that maybe I got pregnant even though I used the diaphragm. And this feeling at first, while I'm in the bliss of love, is the most magnificent feeling, it's like suddenly everything in life is okay at last. But then when I sense that Doug isn't really with me in this feeling, I sometimes freak out, and get all moody, and bum him out I know with my feelings, I even cry sometimes. I know he doesn't want a baby. Well I guess he doesn't, we haven't talked about it for a few months, he's so busy and all. But okay, I admit it—when I come like that, I want to have a baby, that's the bottom line of the situation. And it makes me feel terrible when I feel so empty afterwards."

Another woman, a friend named Angelica who moved to the States with her husband six years ago, and has recently explored new approaches to spiritual and sexual growth, spoke of postorgasm feelings in quite a different way: "The last several years, since Ignacio and I were at Esalen and learned certain things, we've been making love only when we have at least an hour together, and aren't tired or anything. Well sometimes he's still just a bull, you know, and I let him take me fast like in the old days, and then I don't feel much except like a cattle truck just ran over me—but those times are not so often as before, now that he's looking more at his own feelings. Usually he and I lock the door so the kids know we're otherwise engaged, and we just smile at each other with that smile that makes me hungry for him. Then it's like we're coconspirators in some plot, and the challenge is to sneak up upon the sleeping sexual tiger, and by the time we're in bed we're tigers ourselves, we're animals and we're gods at the same time. We more and more learn to take our time. He knows I need to come, and I certainly know he does, that's obvious about two days before he finally gets me. I can feel him like the moon waxing, except that with him it's just about exactly a seven-day cycle, he's just four times as fast as the moon, that man of mine, and I wouldn't want it any less often. I can feel him putting aside his stash of sperm. He starts out depleted from the last time and he's got to go to work breeding the next genera-tion. And me, I know when the egg drops. I'm not a young bird who doesn't know the game. I was forty years old last month and I'm done with having kids, there's four of them already and that's my quota. If you're forty and don't know when your egg drops, you've just missed a big part of the story, let me tell you. It's important to know when the egg drops—ask any woman, 'Is it important to know when your egg drops,' and the young ones will tell you, 'What egg?' But the older you get, unless you've dried up already, it's like a ringing of some interior bell when that egg drops, 'cause some day it won't drop anymore, that's what life is all about. Some day, no more eggs, then some day, no more heartbeats. Life's this steady progression, and what can we do about it? What I do, to be quite honest, is I have at least one orgasm a week that blasts my circuits so wide and high that who cares about having to die, if you've really lived while you had your chance. That's what an orgasm is for me—it makes me feel like I've really lived. It's the same for Ignacio I think. Imagine Ignacio ten years ago letting me talk him into going off to an Esalen weekend retreat way over on the coast, and him being open to this guy sitting there cross-legged talking about orgasms. Now Ignacio's woken up somehow. It wasn't just the workshop, although it helped him more than he admits to hear other men talking about their feelings. Ignacio's a great man, I see this more and more as we make love deeper and deeper. I can see his soul when he just lets go and isn't holding anything back from me anymore, when he's an animal and a god combined. It's like after so long, we've become the dream we had in our minds when we were teenagers. It's a full circle, but at the same time, it's completely different. There's no way to imagine what real love can be like, you've just got to go for it and let it come alive. And for me, that's meant finally accepting Ignacio as my man, and not dreaming anymore of some ideal lover like I used to. Now I've finally let Ignacio be that ideal lover, and the amazing thing is that he is."

The Making of Love

Expressed even in the everyday words we use to describe the sex act between lovers, we discover this mystic notion that love itself is actually generated in the process of engaging in heartfelt sexual encounter. *Love* of course is such an overused, ephemeral term. Let's look a step deeper into what the word actually signifies in our minds and culture.

The spiritual foundation of our present Judeo-Christian civilization has been based for two thousand years on the primary spiritual equation that "God is Love." Jesus taught without question that love is the cornerstone of all things spiritual.

So our personal feelings of love are not isolated events. We are actually participating in a subtle and unifying dimension of energy that pervades life on this planet of ours. Science and religion are finally coming together and pointing toward the unity of all of life, and the existence of a pervading Spirit or unifying principle that holds everything from universe to human body to subatomic particles together in this perfect universal reality.

During lovemaking, our bodies seem to become veritable receiving stations for the energy of love. Our individual isolated membranes dissolve as we approach orgasm, letting love come flooding into us. At a certain point, the opposite energetic poles of male and female bodies flash an arc connecting the two opposite energy systems, and—orgasm!

Each time orgasm is approached, there is this inflowing of energy into our bodies, and then the explosion of this energy in the act of creation. Sometimes when all systems are "go," the orgasm experience generates an actual new physical being in the universe—a baby is created.

And when no baby is created, which is certainly the large majority of the time—what happens to the energies released during orgasm?

It seems that our level of spiritual consciousness at the moment of orgasm determines what happens to this energy that is released. Some people don't build up very much of a charge of energy when making love, and then when they come, the energy just dissipates back into the universal energy source. But as we have been seeing throughout this book, it is quite possible to open our hearts to the inflow of spiritual energy during lovemaking, so that we become transformed, purified, transported into realms of consciousness where direct union with the Spirit, with God, with the Universal Presence, is experienced.

A deeply mystic fellow I have gotten to know in the last few years explained lovemaking in the following way: "This planet isn't everything, we're just an infinitely tiny speck in the universe. But when we let love flow into our hearts, when we let our cells become permeable, when we open ourselves to the Spirit, then we personally serve to bring more love to the planet. We can't really make love, that's a misnomer. What we can do is to open up and receive it. Hearts can be closed, hearts can be open. It's as simple as that. And when hearts are open, bodies fill up with love, there's no effort, it's the natural human condition. Then when the body, every cell in the body, is charged with love, this energy can radiate out and still be replaced so there's no energy loss, even when there's a great amount of love flowing out and into other hearts. Imagine Jesus, here's a human being who was unbelievably charged with love, and at the same time, He was spreading unbelievable amounts of love to everyone around him. It's true. The more you give, the more you receive. That's the basic law of love. And if you don't give any, you don't have any, either. That's what Jesus meant when He said that those who have, will receive more, but those who don't have, will lose even what they do have. Giving means having."

The Neuropsychology of Love

Let's look in a supposedly opposite direction from religious insight for a few moments, and see what science has to say these days about the pharmacology of love. In the old Newtonian way of viewing the human body, in which everything was seen as an automatic biochemical process, scientists were able to explain away the power of love by simply pointing out in more and more sophisticated detail the ways in which various brain chemicals affect emotional states of mind and body. "People in the first flush of falling in love," Lawrence Crapo in *Hormones, The Messenger of Life* states, "generate large quantities of arousing brain drugs such as phenylethylamine, dopamine, and norepinephrine. The essential link between sexual desire and neurochemicals has been well established."

Thus it is possible to assume logically that everything we feel and think while making love is purely a product of our own internal biochemical functioning. If indeed we are isolated biological organisms as was previously assumed in science, then it would seem reasonable to say that love isn't anything more than a glandular assortment of biological secretions. I remember being taught this very assumption as solid fact when I was in grad school in psychology—that there is no Spirit, that there is no external shared experience while making love. There is only the internal experience that we then project outward onto our lover, the universe, and God.

Now however, with so many radical breakthroughs in subatomic physics and quantum mechanics, scientists are finally realizing that there is a level of reality way beyond the mechanistic view of Newtonian science. In fact, as such scientific journalists as Dorion Sagan in *Biospheres* and Rudy Rucker in *Infinity and the Mind* have recently explained in lay terms, the universe simply cannot function without an underlying sense of connectedness and consciousness permeating the universe and perhaps beyond the universe. The mystic notion of Spirit is becoming a scientific notion of connectedness and transpersonal consciousness.

When two people are attracted to each other, this attraction can be realistically seen as both biochemical sexual hunger and at the same time a higher-level bioelectronic and biomagnetic phenomenon, in which the two persons are actually merging their personal identities on a vast number of subtle fronts, most of them beyond the scope of normal consciousness.

We know of the vast power of the atom when two sub-atomic particles merge. Unbelieveable energy is released. In some similar energetic way, when two human beings come together through mutual attraction, and step by step increase their personal charge of energy as they approach sexual intimacy, a transpersonal charge is built up between the two bodies and bioenergetic systems.

Orgasm releases this charge. Opposites (male and female) are united for a short time. And with this flash of energetic transference comes the power of creation into biochemical realms of everyday human life. The universe for a moment is experienced consciously as being united through human love. And while in this infinitely expansive state of awareness, two lovers know directly the presence of the Spirit that permeates all of life.

Aftermath of Creation

A man can ejaculate, feel the biochemical rush that is generated by ejaculation, and then very soon drop down to normal again as if nothing has happened. If there is not also the power of love permeating a sexual encounter, not much energy remains after coming. This is the reality of making love with the genitals, and not allowing the inflow of creative energy to rise up through the rest of the body, as the Kundalini model we discussed earlier shows.

A woman has a somewhat different postorgasm experience. Even during masturbation, a woman will have a longer aftermath than a man. This makes perfect sense when we consider that for the man, the moment of ejaculation is his high point, but for the woman, the physical act of creation requires more time, while the sperm swim gallantly toward the source, hoping to reach the female egg and bring about the act of creation.

For a woman, remaining in bliss, in contact with the Spirit, with the universe itself, for a longer time means that she will hopefully still have her personal consciousness merged with the universal consciousness when the act of conception occurs. This is one explanation for the female orgasm response in contrast to the male ejaculation experience.

Struggling to stick our own personal orgasm and postorgasm experience into the realm of science at this point ultimately proves fruitless, however. No scientific explanation portrays the full extent of any of life. Science is ultimately a set of concepts that attempts to describe reality, but these concepts are not reality. It is only when we personally go through the crucial expansion process that moves us into direct mystic interface with the greater reality beyond our personal minds that we come to know for ourselves the reality of the unified wholeness of all of life.

This seems to be the love experience, this expanding beyond our personal boundaries so as to include someone else in our bubble, and in extension to experience consciously our isolated selves as a part of the All. Orgasm is the peak of this experience, and the postorgasm experience is the blessing of remaining in bliss and oneness for at least a few minutes after orgasm, enabling us to integrate this mystic experience into our everyday consciousness.

You have probably experienced quite a number of postorgasm moments and minutes of bliss and altered consciousness. Let me give you time now to employ your own "in-bed research data" to give you a better understanding of how you personally relate with feelings that arise after co-itus. After reading this paragraph, you can put the book aside if you want to and look first to your present-moment breathing experience . . . your whole body alive and charged with a certain amount of love and life force right now . . . and while you remain attuned with your present feelings, let your mind look back and relive the last time you made love . . . what was your orgasm and postorgasm experience . . . what actually happened energetically between you and your lover.

Prolonging the Bliss Experience

We all have our habits regarding what to do after coming. Usually, these habits were established early in our lovemak-ing experience and were therefore caught up in a certain nervousness about how to relate with our lover after sharing such an intense experience together.

By and large, what most of us do after orgasm is go to work reassembling our old ego and sense of self so that we can carry on as functional folks in everyday interactions. If we make love at night and just fall asleep afterward, of course the process is mostly effortless. We drift into dreams and sleep, and when we wake up in the morning, we carry on.

But if we make love and then continue relating with our lover, or get up and go about our day, we are more conscious of the way in which orgasm has affected us. We can feel the effects of spiritual merging, and either react against it so as to save our old sense of who we are or allow the essential growth and transformation process to happen to us.

The thrust of this book is of course that it is to our

advantage to encourage consciously a reassembling of our sense of who we are, so that the inflow of love and insight during lovemaking has a positive effect on our overall life. This is how we use the energy of lovemaking for positive growth.

How specifically can this postcoital growth process be encouraged?

The same principles that applied before intercourse and during intercourse apply after intercourse equally. As you have seen, there is a unifying principle to all the sexual meditations I have taught in this book. The principle is simple: We must learn to pause and expand our awareness of the present moment if we are to reap the benefits of the present moment. I have simply taught variations on this basic "power of attention" theme.

The main detrimental habit most of us carry around inside us comes into action right after orgasm, that of immediately shifting into the thought mode. Our minds go to work trying to make sense of what we have experienced. Fearing the overwhelming power of pure bliss, the conceptual part of our identity tries to regain dominance as soon as possible after intercourse. And as soon as we start thinking, we lose the magic of the mystic moment we have attained during intercourse.

So you will want to observe your habits in this regard. Notice what your mind does after you come. See these conditioned patterns in action the next few times you make love, without trying to alter them. Become conscious of your mind's reflex reactions to orgasm.

Then you can apply the techniques you already know for freeing yourself from mental dominance. This means consciously staying aware of your breathing and the feelings in your body after you come, rather than losing awareness of this vital dimension where the Spirit can touch your soul.

Indulge in the rush of the hormones through your nervous system and cellular consciousness. Ride the tide of postorgasm bliss wherever it wants to take you—this is the trick!

By breaking you free of habitual thought flows and mind games, orgasm puts you in position to have a completely new experience of what it means to be alive on this planet, in love with someone you can share sexual intimacies with—and, at least for a few minutes, free of pressures that demand your attention. Right after coming, you are in position to surrender to the magic of transpersonal consciousness even more than during intercourse. Who knows what will come to you?

"Sometimes I have these amazing flashings of colors that seem to fill me up," one man described. "It's unbelievable—I actually become color. And the color is pulsating, alive. Then sometimes all I'm aware of is my body, I'm nothing but my body. It's hard to describe, but I feel like I'm gigantic, and the feeling is absolutely delicious. I wouldn't call it spiritual, it's just pure sensation, pure being—which I guess is spiritual too. And there are all these flashes of vague memories of moments from my past when I felt the bliss, when I felt similar to how I feel after coming these days. Sometimes images come to mind that wake up such strong feelings. It's like the past and the present are together. Even sometimes I think the future is there too. The whole notion of time goes away when I have a deep sexual time. That's what makes orgasm special, it's a liberation from time. And it doesn't just get that way when I come. From the very first minutes when we're in bed and the passion hits, that's when orgasm begins for me, and I can stay in that high state all during the beginnings. When I first go into her, that's coming for me, there's an ultimate moment when I first slide into her that's just as overwhelming as when I come, some-

times more overwhelming, because by the time I actually
ejaculate I feel like I've come ten, twenty times. The whole
experience is one spread-out coming from my inside point
of view."

"There are feelings that rise up in me that come from
nowhere," a woman explained. "They're maybe out of some
book I've read about mythology, I don't know, or from
what Carl Jung called the collective unconscious. I think
there's some truth to all that mythic talk. But I sometimes
see visions, as if I'm one of the visions myself, and they're
these perfect beings, gods, in perfect harmony with each
other. It sounds silly when I talk about it, which is why I
don't talk about it very often, but that's what happens to
me after I come. For a few minutes at least, I'm off in some
dreamland, completely gone, and yet completely there. Jack
and I like just to lie side by side afterward. Usually, I come
after he does, and then we bliss out together. The strange
thing is that sometimes there's no feeling of being myself—
I'm Jack and me together, we're in this dreamland, but I've
never talked with him about it. I don't know if he has the
same visions. That's the kind of thing that's hard to talk
about with him. We don't talk much at all right afterward
usually, and then once we're up and out of bed, such talk
seems foolish."

"I like to sit up after coming, after a couple of minutes of
just slowly letting me get small and come out of her," a male
client told me. "If I lie down too long I get strange and dizzy,
it's too much. But if I sit up after a real strong experience in
bed, then I can stay in the feelings and that's great. It's like
I'm still coming somewhere inside me, up and down my
spine mostly. Norma usually lies there just blissed out a
while longer, and then she sits up too, and we usually smoke
a cigarette together and talk. We can talk real deep after

coming. That's when we talk best, sometimes for hours. We both feel full of energy and relaxed at the same time, it's the best feeling."

"Sometimes I can't help myself, I just get this deep yearning feeling inside me after coming, as if I've just been with some deep friend when making love, and then as the flush of orgasm wears off, I feel I'm slipping away from this love I've contacted, and sometimes I even cry. Richard holds me and that's so good, he has such a big heart, he even gets tears sometimes, too. It's not crying for any particular reason, I'm actually happy deep down when I'm crying like that. But there's such an immense pressure inside me, so much love, and I just have to cry. Then afterward I turn into just the opposite—I'm up and laughing, tears still streaming down my cheeks. It's such an overwhelming experience when we really go into it so deeply that I've just got to cry and laugh afterward sometimes. Is that normal?"

There are of course no normalcy standards for how to feel and behave after coming. The only rule of thumb is the "spontaneity" rule we've been exploring all along. What we can hope for is the blessing of a lover who gives us the space to express our feelings spontaneously after lovemaking, so that we feel free to explore new levels of consciousness. And, of course, we must give ourselves permission as well—and grant this permission to our lover in turn.

Many men confess to sometimes being afraid of how their partners react after orgasm. The flooding of female emotions can be scary. "It used to make me afraid that she was going crazy," one man explained. "Just out of the blue, she'd get hit with some strong feeling, sometimes she'd burst out crying, right while we were making love or afterward. And I'd think that I'd done something wrong, or that she didn't feel satisfied being with me. It took me a while before I learned what was really going on inside her. Now I don't mind, I even kind of like it. She wakes up feelings inside myself that I usually don't let myself feel, just those sad feelings, you know, all the lonely feelings that I felt when I was a kid I guess and didn't let myself feel back then. They come welling up inside me when Caroline lets go and cries. Sometimes I'm crying in her arms too. That's something I never thought would happen to me. I was brought up not to be a sissy. But I feel strong after I cry."

Emotion Unto Spirit

The discharge of strong feelings right after making love, or in the middle of making love, is one of the universal occurrences lovers note throughout the world and throughout history. I have spoken of the beautiful cathartic value of this emotional release experience. Old heartbreaks are allowed to heal; forbidden feelings are allowed expression. We discover depths to our own hearts that we never knew existed before.

It is usually only after the emotional dimensions and pressures are vented and relieved that more spiritual feelings are able to rise up in the heart. This is why it is so important to give your lover permission to feel bad feelings after coming sometimes, so that the essential heart healing can take place. And, of course, you must really trust your lover if you are to open up and express negative feelings after making love. This is one of the primary values of an enduring relationship—that step by step we can trust enough to open up buried feelings that otherwise remain under the surface all our lives, distorting our experience of life because they are not given release.

I strongly encourage you to reflect upon this aspect of lovemaking, and consciously to give your lover more and more permission to break down during and after lovemaking. Give yourself this permission, as well. It takes time. Don't push. But after coming, relax and open up the essential time and space and emotional trust so that spontaneous emotional flows can happen.

Often after coming, there isn't any emotional charge at all to be released. The process of orgasm blows away the charge quite cleanly. But sometimes, there remains a charge. To relax and feel if there is a charge, and to let it come out if it is there—this is true sexual maturity.

A key method for allowing this release is the "jaw relaxation" exercise I mentioned in Chapter Three (see page 73). Emotions are held within us chronically by keeping the mouth closed and jaws tight. After coming, see what happens if you consciously just lie there on your back, focus on your breathing and the pressures in your chest, and breathe through your mouth. As Wilhelm Reich first pointed out, emotional release and healing often require this experience of breathing through the mouth. Emotions are, after all, released primarily through breathing and vocalization, along with whole-body movements. If you consciously make the physical step of relaxing the jaw and tongue and breathing through the mouth, you put yourself into perfect position for emotional discharge and healing.

Experiment with this right now if you want to. Just let your jaw relax, breathe through your mouth, close your eyes after finishing reading this paragraph, and notice what feelings might instantly rise up inside you, and if you have any emotional charge within you, give yourself permission to express these feelings in a spontaneous way.

Surrendering to the Divine

Because of unfortunate childhood experiences and instruction, many people are chronically afraid of spiritual feelings that can come rushing into their bodies. These people often use a distorted form of emotional busyness and discharge to keep them from ever encountering themselves beyond the confines of their habitual emotional consciousness. The truth is that spiritual consciousness arises within us when our emotional charges are finally and at least temporarily released. We must surrender our identity as emotional beings as well as cognitive beings if we are to advance into purely mystic realms of consciousness.

As I'm sure you've noticed, many people seem to be caught up in one emotion or another during almost all their waking moments. They're either upset about something, worried about something, excited about something; they keep themselves charged with emotion throughout the day. When their environment doesn't provoke an emotion, their minds and imaginings do the job. There is never any peace, never any calmness to their minds—never any chance for transcendent flashes to jolt them with the realization that there is a mysterious dimension to life, quite beyond their chronic emotional and mental condition.

Probably at least 90 percent of our everyday emotional traumas are generated not by the environment stimulating certain feelings directly but by the activities of our own mental habits as they run chronic thoughts through our minds that, in turn, stimulate various emotions. In this way, we can be emotional junkies as easily as thought junkies—and we keep our minds engaged in order to avoid encounter with the mysterious infinite realms of consciousness that lie beyond our personal egos.

You can begin to evaluate you own habits in this regard. Do you go around thinking thoughts that generate emotional trauma inside you a great deal of the time, or do you often allow your feelings to be calm, your mind quiet, so that your soul can come alive?

Surrendering to sexual passion, when it is a genuine surrender, is by definition a letting go of all these habitual games the mind plays, so that true communion with our deeper nature can be experienced. One of the main reasons we tend to crave sexual encounter is because it does force us to let go and transcend normal consciousness.

But right after coming, what do we do? Do we allow ourselves to remain in bliss, or do we almost instantly go back into our normal mental gears? In essence, are we at home in spiritual realms of bliss such as come to us after orgasm, or are we afraid of these mystic states, habitually running away from them?

In your next few sexual encounters, begin to observe this in yourself. Do you use or abuse your emotional nature, for instance? Do you relax into bliss after coming, or quickly void the transcendent experience through reactivating your thinking mind? And do you breathe into the vastness of your spiritual identity, or run away from it?

Pause again now at the end of this chapter, and reflect on this important theme of how you respond to the mystic opportunities that arise right after orgasm.

FINAL WORDS:
Transcendence Through Earthly Love

Through the course of this book, we have been exploring how the spirit of mystic love can be encouraged to come flooding into the physical act of sexual surrender, through the expansion of our intimate interactions in seven primary dimensions. Now that we have gained various insights into the seven aspects of enhanced spiritual sexuality, we are in a position to look back and see the whole that encompasses the separate pieces of the sexual puzzle.

I experienced this whole as I awoke this morning to the sound of a rooster crowing outside my window. I lay in bed quietly for a few minutes, letting my dreams flow through my mind while my waking body slowly came into focus. I could feel myself alive, feel my heartbeat, feel my breaths coming and going, feel my whole body as a living presence on the planet, just as the rooster could feel his own earthly presence, just as everyone in my community waking up to a new day on planet Earth could feel alive in the new morning.

This direct sensory quality of aliveness is what makes possible the entire range of human experience. If we do not feel alive in our bodies, there is no hope of experiencing any of the supposedly higher states of consciousness. We must first be aware of our primal earthly presence in our own personal body.

What we have been seeing in this book by looking concertedly at the actual experience of sexual love is that as human beings, we come to know our spiritual depths by opening ourselves totally to our earthly instinctual feelings and actions. By becoming 100 percent physical, we become 100 percent divine. By surrendering completely to our primal sexual desires and earthly yearnings, we come face-to-face with the creative force that animates all of life.

This earthly path to spiritual awakening is of course what Jesus, Lao Tzu, and Buddha were teaching—that our challenge as human beings is to manifest our ultimate earthly presence, and, by so doing, to discover the spiritual foundations that underlie physical life. Jesus was teaching us that what He could do, we could do also. He was offering us a clear example of what it means to be fully human.

My hope is that we are now emerging into a period of history where we finally stop playing out the conceptual game of positing one opposite against another, and taking sides with one or the other. Wholeness needs to become our primary motto in life. And this wholeness means the realization that our instinctual animal nature is as holy as our lofty spiritual nature—and that through merging heaven and earth, we attain our true identity.

The earliest mention of wholeness that I have found in world literature is perhaps the deepest in this regard. It is found in an ancient book written by a Chinese wise man named Lao Tzu, entitled *Tao Te Ching*, or "book of the way." He speaks of wholeness as follows:

> *These things from ancient times arise from one:*
> *The sky is whole and clear.*
> *The earth is whole and firm.*
> *The spirit is whole and strong.*
> *The valley is whole and full.*
> *The ten thousand things are whole and alive.*
> *Kings and lords are whole, and the country is upright.*
> *All these are in virtue of wholeness.*

David Bohm, one of the primary scientists of our era, a physicist carrying on in the basic tradition of Albert Einstein, has come to the same basic conclusion as Lao Tzu did, when he concludes that "inseparable quantum interconnectedness of the whole universe is the fundamental reality."

What we have been exploring in this book is how all human beings are organically endowed with the capacity to make direct contact with this "inseparable quantum interconnectedness," this mystic unity of all of life. Our primary everyday vehicle for experiencing the feeling of wholeness in our lives is, as we have seen, that of regular surrender to the infinite joys of sexual encounter with our loved one. This is where instinct and spirit merge in a purely spontaneous way in human life. There are other meditational paths to spiritual awakening surely, where sexual intercourse is not employed. But for most of us, the sexual path is the most direct, the easiest to attain, and, well, the most enjoyable!

As I lay in bed this morning, I could feel directly the basic life force within me. I knew I was alive because of this vital energetic power animating my awareness. I felt what is usually called a zest for life, a thrill at waking up into another unique day on planet Earth. The rooster crowed again.

Without effort I found myself getting up from bed, eager to be in action.

Every movement was a pleasure to me, as long as I didn't push, as long as I stayed with my breathing, with my whole body, and didn't get sucked into the tug of my "planning and plotting" thinking mind and thus pulled out of the present moment. I found my door opening and my wife coming in for a morning hug and kiss (we too like to sleep apart most of the time to keep our relationship hot and fresh), and the sexual energy in my body rose up for a few minutes of overt sexual encounter. But having made love the day before, and having our little one pressing his body between our legs for attention, we easily put aside our direct sexual energies, and joined our spirits as three in the wholeness of our family circle.

Now an hour later, I am doing what I have done throughout the writing of this book, which is to remain in my body, remain in the present moment of my feelings and physical presence, while also reflecting in written form at the computer, so that communication is possible with those of you whom I do not know personally. The primal power of sexual energy continues to flow through my body, the life force animates my every action and thought and feeling, regardless of what I am doing. My challenge is to remain conscious of the actual experience of being alive in every new moment. This is, of course, your challenge, too.

My point is this: Sexual energy is not just something that rises up in the heat of sexual intercourse and disappears the rest of the time. This basic creative energy animates everything we do, as I have mentioned several times in different contexts in this book, and in other books as well. And the final thought I want to offer to you is this—that you become more and more conscious of the fact that your instinctive sexual energy does empower you through every moment of every day. There is in fact a wholeness to your life experience, and this wholeness is felt through the continuity of the flow of the life force through your body.

You are always, in essence, making love, if you are consciously alive and participating in the flow of the life force. This is why, for instance, my wife and I usually only make love about once a week these days, after seven years together. We were like most lovers and made love almost every day when we were first together. But we have learned as the years have gone by how to spread our sexual energies out into everything we do, so that there is a feeling of empowerment and passion in every act, every social encounter, every moment of playing with our new son or doing work of any nature.

Especially when a couple creates a new being, much of the sexual energy of that couple that previously went into direct sexual intercourse becomes shifted and is directed to the new creature on the planet. This is how sexual love instinctively spreads itself, expands its territory, and nurtures the development of the new generation.

It is the same with any type of life's work that offers you the chance to express yourself lovingly and creatively in the world. You put your heart and soul into your work—and the energy that motivates this work is also the primal sexual energy of creation.

Likewise, the soul also needs regular times of retreat and solitary reflection, or meditation, if you will. And again, during meditation, we tap into the basic life force that animates us, and use this energy to fuel our mystic meditative experiences.

When we consciously participate in the life force in everything we do, we create a sense of wholeness in our lives. In essence, we spread love wherever we go. As Ken Keyes has pointed out in his *Handbook to Higher Consciousness*, it is a major mistake to focus too much attention on genital stimulation and release, to make overt orgasm the great goal and only glory of a relationship. In fact, as I have found through my work as a therapist over the years, people who are genitally fixated are usually quite unhappy, unsatisfied people, because they don't yet know how to let their sexual energies move into their entire bodies and lives. Instead, they know only how to let the energy flow through the genitals to discharge—without the heart getting activated in the process.

We have explored a primary path in this book for consciously encouraging the sexual energies to break free of genital fixations, and to flood the heart and the other energy centers of the body with love and light, with power and spiritual clarity. I hope you have come to appreciate this process in its simplicity and also its pragmatic power of transformation.

In one of Bob Dylan's early songs, he makes a poetic point that has resonated in my mind ever since first hearing it on one of his records back in 1966—his gravelly voice claiming that everyone's either busy being born or busy dying. This statement seems to be the heart of the human experience, expressing once again the basic teaching of Jesus—that the underlying dynamic of life is a constant rebirth process, in which we let go of the past, open ourselves to the unique impetus of the present moment, and spontaneously grow into a newness that brings us alive, that lets the Spirit come into our hearts and minds and enable us to live life to the utmost.

We are in fact always in the process of being born. Birth doesn't end with our physical emergence from the womb. We are constantly becoming new—if we remain conscious, if we stay in tune with the eternal present, if we open our hearts to the mystic dimensions of life. And when we make love, we have the ultimate opportunity to let go of our egos, to die to the past, and, through orgasm or even just through sexual closeness, to experience the rebirth of our spirit into a new creation.

The Very Next Step

I would like to turn your attention, here at the end of the written discussion, to the ongoing cycle of sexual excitation and discharge that punctuates your own life. Your intimate bouts of lovemaking with your mate or lover obviously occur in a cyclic pattern, timewise. At some point after your last sexual encounter, your body and soul begin hungering again for the special closeness and pleasure of sexual intercourse, for shared intimacy and orgastic discharge and bliss. This rising charge inside you begins to attract your lover to you, especially since he or she will probably be feeling this increase in sexual charge and attraction at about the same time as you are.

For some time, both of you probably direct your charge of positive creative energy into other things besides intercourse. If you are at work, you are a bright light unto the world, a shining image of sexual vitality. If you are alone, your reflective thoughts and bodily feelings will be amplified by the surging power of desire in your nervous system. If you are with your children, if you have any, you will find yourself full of energy, playful, physically warm, and compassionate.

Then at some point you do come together with your lover and make love, discharging the specific genital pressures you were feeling, and hopefully charging your spiritual batteries in the process. Following the lovemaking, usually there is a period of little or no sexual desire and charge. Then the whole thing starts over again.

Right when you begin to feel a renewal of your sexual hungers for intimacy and intercourse, it is important to tune into these feelings, and consciously observe them all the way to orgasm and beyond, if you want to fully tap into the blessings of sexual love. Many people, partly because of negative programmings during puberty, ignore and even actively avoid acknowledging their own sexual feelings, and those of their lover or mate, until the pressure is so great it can't be pushed underground any longer. This denial of the preliminary phases of sexual arousal tends to diffuse and distort the pure inflow of love energy that comes on a regular basis to human beings involved in a sexual relationship.

We are sexual beings. Therefore to deny the first budding pressures to express this sexual energy overtly through intercourse and orgasm is to deny our very essence. A great many of us act out this self-denial routine on a regular basis, however. We habitually react with shame, with guilt, with subtle apprehension when we feel deep within our own bodies the rising hunger to go ape, to go animal, to rip off our clothes and jump into bed with a member of the opposite sex.

I encourage you to develop the transformational habit of regularly observing yourself in action in this regard, to see how you personally were conditioned to react to your beginning feelings of renewed sexual desire. See how your childhood programmings are still influencing the ways in which you either open up and allow sexual energy to flow into your body toward a new orgasm experience or close down and try to deny and block this beautiful pleasure-oriented rush of sexual desire wanting to take over your body.

It used to be that religious training in our culture associated the rising of sexual desire with the work of the devil himself. In fact, the devil in medieval times was usually portrayed as a sexually potent half-animal creature who shamelessly showed his sexual energy and charge, and thus awakened this sinful feeling of animal lust in the hearts and genitals of the unwary.

The truth is that as the body regularly repeats its sexual-appetite cycle, certain biochemical changes do happen at glandular levels in the brain, and these changes do tend to drive us a bit batty. If we are afraid of our own sexual energies, when we feel a surge of sexual desire rush through our bodies, provoking emotions, thoughts, and fantasies that seem completely unrelated to whatever busywork we are engaged in at the moment, it can feel exactly as if we are being possessed by the devil himself.

If we don't contract against this flush of sexual desire, however, we don't have to get knocked off center by it. In fact, we can learn step by step, as is done in Kundalini training, for example, to ride the sexual energies with perfect balance, doing our regular routines in life while getting higher and higher on the biochemical as well as the more mystic dynamics of physical love and desire.

In *The Act of Creation*, Arthur Koestler described how great artists, leaders, athletes, and lovers alike masterfully tap into this rush of sexual power and desire, and ride this energy in the directions they so choose. There seems to be only one basic creative energy, and if we are afraid to let it flood into us, if we fear being overwhelmed by it, then we chronically tend to hold ourselves at low levels of energetic excitation and we are depressed, uncreative, noncharismatic, and usually quite bored with life. Boredom is, in fact, a direct blocking of the inflow of sexual excitement into the body.

Even when we are sitting quietly doing nothing, we are

in the act of creation—we are creating a basic feeling inside us, which is then broadcast out into our environment. If we are letting our feelings and thoughts flow spontaneously, if we are allowing our body to charge with energy and to flow with that charge of energy effortlessly, then we will be creating a beautiful aura of love and acceptance, of power and grace, around us wherever we go and whatever we do.

The act of creation, therefore, is, not just an overt sexual act or an obvious making of something or other. We are busy creating ourselves, every minute of the day. More to the point, either we are allowing the perfect grace and love and light of the universe to permeate our being or we are interfering with this natural process.

See what happens if you pause now for just one minute of your life, and after putting the book aside, observe whether you are open right now to the inflow of the life force into your body and being, or whether you are by habit resisting this effortless creative inflow of the Spirit into your personal awareness.

Your Next Sexual Encounter

In concluding, let me give you an overview of the main points we have been exploring, so that you have a concrete format for continuing to observe yourself as you move toward your very next sexual encounter. Please hold in mind that we have covered a great deal of material in just one book, and you will almost certainly want to go back and do many of the exercises and reflective meditations a number of times in order to master the seven steps we have explored.

Here is the basic path to sexual and spiritual "wholeness"

that we have explored in this book. Taking this brief sketch as your format, see in the next hours and days how you tend to express or repress your sexual feelings as you progress toward the very next, and quite possibly the very best, sexual encounter of your life to date:

1. Notice first of all the extent to which you find yourself drifting back into your past, reliving experiences with past lovers and friends, trying to rework traumas and confusions that linger in your heart. Are you free to be with your current lover in the eternal present moment, or is your heart somehow still hung up with an old flame from the past?

2. As the energy for sexual passion rises up inside you in the next hours and days, do you tend to reach for a beer or some other chemical means of altering the sexual power of your body, or do you ride the rising tide of sexual desires with a clear mind and sensitive neurological system?

3. What does your voice tell you and your lover about your true feelings? Are you sincerely broadcasting your sexual desires when speaking with your lover, or do you try to hide your growing passions? Do you release your inner feelings when you speak, or choke the feelings back? And when you finally reach climax, does your voice vibrate with the power of the spirit of sexual love, or is it afraid to express your soul-felt emotions?

4. As you next encounter your lover, notice the ways in which your eyes either look and make contact or avoid visual intercourse. Can you instantly penetrate your lover with your eyes and experience the flash of sexual energy that can happen between two charged nervous systems or are you still afraid of this level of intimacy?

5. Then comes touching. Perhaps at first, you don't touch at all. Notice whether you are conscious of the powerful emotions that can be generated by the slightest touch when you and your lover are just beginning to hunger for each other. Observe the patterns of touching, of kissing, of hugging, of fondling each other that you presently share. See whether you can breathe into spontaneous skin-to-skin exchanges that have never happened before. Remember often that you can pause in whatever you might be doing sexually with your lover, and take a breather. Notice how it feels sometimes to drop back to the beginning levels of sensitivity while engaged in sexual intercourse. See whether you can observe what your mind habitually does, not only when you are in bed with your lover but even in the first twinges of sexual desire, long before skin-to-skin relating comes about again. To what extent does your thinking mind allow itself to participate in the whole-body experience of sexual arousal, and to what extent does your thinking mind run away from your natural sexual feelings?

6. Also right from the beginning, notice if and when the rising of sexual desire in your body stimulates the flow of fantasies through your mind. Do you sometimes wake up with wild sexual dreams fresh in your mind, for instance? Do you walk down the street feeling energetic rushes of sexual desire in your muscles as you walk, and suddenly glance at a handsome or beautiful body and imagine all sorts of sexual things happening between you? How does your fantasy mind deal with the inflow of sexual desire into your nervous system, and how successfully do you put aside this fantasy as you approach orgasm?

7. Finally, we come to the orgasm experience in action. Perhaps the best way to grasp the true nature of spiritual orgasm is to expand the concept of orgasm itself. Orgasm is not just the sudden peak point of climax. Orgasm begins with that first tiny flush of sexual desire that comes into your mind and body, hours, days, or perhaps even weeks before the actual explosion of sexual climax might hit you. Orgasm is a bell curve that begins to rise up as your sexual batteries start to develop a new charge, and continues to rise up to the climax point, perhaps with five, ten, or fifty miniclimaxes before the final discharge. Both men and women have these smaller orgasmic sensations of release many times before genital discharge occurs. And afterward, the orgasm continues for some time, if allowed to linger.

Then desire is temporarily down, sexual interest almost nil, the muse of passion gone from our bodies for awhile in most cases. Sometimes passion will rise up again in just a few minutes. Many women would like to ride the orgasm express for a seemingly endless number of orgasms in the same lovemaking session. Men in particular tend to release all their steam in one ejaculation, and to need half an hour, a day, a few days before the charge is high again. This of course is not true of men who practice the fine art of not coming at all, of holding their seed, and experiencing spiritual orgasm over and over again with their lover without ejaculating. This is perhaps an ideal, but for most men not a regular sexual practice. The down period is therefore a regular experience, and should be appreciated as well. It allows the charging of the spiritual batteries as well as the repopulation of the genitals with little swimmers.

With Reverence and Awe

What seems most important to hold in mind in conclusion is the ongoing challenge of nurturing a greater sense of continual awe and reverence for the very presence of the sexual charge within our bodies, and within the bodies of those we encounter. We are all sexually charged. We are all continually learning how to manage this precious charge at more successful levels in our everyday lives. To acknowledge this basic fact of life is to raise the level of consciousness of human exchange to new heights of compassion and understanding.

Many of us tend to ignore the sexual presence of people we meet, since we are afraid of what our response would be if we clearly acknowledged the sexuality of other people. But the truth is that we don't have to jump on everyone we encounter just because we observe and appreciate their personal sexual presence.

What we actually observe when we see the sexual creative force emanating from the presence of another human being is the Spirit that animates all of life. When we learn to see God in our sexual desires, when we see the Spirit in action in our hunger for intimacy, when we see love blossoming as sexual potency, then we will interact with this sexual energy in ways that nurture the whole soul of the person we are encountering. We will be able to participate in the sexual aura of everyone we meet, share the level of intimacy and friendship that is proper for the moment with that person, and actually touch that person's heart with our heart through the power of sexual love.

When sexuality is approached as it has been in this book, very little promiscuity actually occurs. The reason some people chronically jump from one bed to another is usually because they are not able to satisfy themselves at deep-enough levels sexually. Once true satisfaction is gained with one person, there is a beautiful sense of sexual potency in everything one does and with everyone one encounters, without there being the desire for direct sexual charging and discharge with anyone but the most intimate sexual friend.

Therefore we can spread our love, we can radiate sexual presence and joy, we can be the beautiful creatures we were intended to be—and still be faithful, trustworthy, and dedicated to our true love.

BIBLIOGRAPHY

Bancroft, J. *Biological Determinants of Sexual Behavior*. Chichester, England: John Wiley and Sons, 1978.

Barbach, L. *For Yourself: The Fulfillment of Female Sexuality*. New York: Signet, 1975.

Bennett, J. G. *Sex, The Relationship Between Sex and Spiritual Development*. York Beach, Maine: Samuel Weiser, 1981.

Castaneda, C. *Tales of Power*. New York: Simon and Schuster, 1974.

Chang, J. *The Tao of Love and Sex*. New York: Dutton, 1986.

Chia, M. *Cultivating Female Sexual Energy*. New York: Morrow, 1986.

———. *Taoist Secrets of Love*. Santa Fe: Aurora Press, 1984.

Crapo, L. *Hormones, the Messenger of Life*. New York: Freeman, 1985.

De Rougement, D. *Love in the Western World*. New York: Pantheon Books, 1956.

Ehrenreich, B. et al. *Remaking Love: The Feminization of Sex*. New York: Doubleday, 1986.

Ellis, H. *Sex Without Guilt*. Hollywood: Wilshire Books, 1966.

———. *Studies in the Psychology of Sex*. New York: Random House, 1942.

Eysenck, H. *Sex and Personality*. London: Open Books, 1979.

Ford, C. S. *Patterns of Sexual Behavior*. New York: Harper, 1951.

Freud, S. "Three Essays on the Theory of Sexuality" in *The Basic Writings of Sigmund Freud*. London: Hogarth Press, 1953–64.

Friday, N. *My Secret Garden: Women's Sexual Fantasies*. New York: Pocket Books, 1974.

Fromm, E. *The Art of Loving*. New York: Bantam, 1963.

Gerrard, M. *Males and Sexuality*. Albany: State University of New York Press, 1987.

Golas, T. *The Lazy Man's Guide to Enlightenment*. New York: Bantam, 1980.

Grant, V. *Psychology of Sexual Emotion*. New York: Longmans, 1957.

Griffett, W. *Males, Females and Sexuality*. Albany: State University of New York, 1987.

Hirsch, E. *The Power to Love*. New York: Pyramid, 1961.

Hutchison, M. *The Anatomy of Sex and Power*. New York: Morrow, 1990.

Kazantzakis, N. *Zorba the Greek*. New York: Ballantine, 1952.

Kinsey, A. C. et al. *Sexual Behavior in the Human Male*. Philadelphia: Saunders, 1948.

Kramer, J. *The Passionate Mind*. Milbrae, CA: Celestial Arts, 1974.

Krishnamurti, J. *The Flame of Attention*. New York: Harper, 1984.

Lowen, A. *Love, Sex and Your Heart*. New York: Macmillan, 1988.

———. *The Spirituality of the Body*. New York: Macmillan, 1990.

Maccoby, E., and Jacklin, C. *The Psychology of Sex Differences*. Palo Alto, CA: Stanford University Press, 1974.

Mead, M. *Male and Female*. New York: Morrow, 1974.

Pearce, J. C. *Magical Child Matures*. New York: Bantam, 1986.

Pierrakos, E. *The Pathwork of Self-Transformation*. New York: Bantam, 1990.

Rajneesh, B. *The Book of the Secrets*. Antelope, OR: Rajneesh Foundation, 1976.

Reich, W. *The Function of the Orgasm*. New York: Orgone Institute Press, 1948; New York: Farrar, Straus & Giroux, 1973.

———. *The Sexual Revolution*. New York: Farrar, Straus & Giroux, 1945.

Selby, J. *Finding Each Other*. London: Element Books, 1988.

———. *Kundalini Awakening*. New York: Bantam, 1992.

———. *Secrets of a Good Night's Sleep*. New York: Avon Books, 1989.

———. *The Visual Handbook*. London: Element Books, 1987.

Symons, D. *The Evolution of Human Sexuality*. New York: Oxford University Press, 1979.

Taylor, G. *Sex in History*. London: Thames and Hudson, 1954.

Watts, A. *Nature, Man and Woman*. New York: Vintage, 1958.

Wilson, G. *Love and Instinct*. New York: Morrow, 1981.